Fēmálè

Fēmálè

DEVIN
IZZARD

PALMETTO
P U B L I S H I N G
Charleston, SC
www.PalmettoPublishing.com

Paperback ISBN: 9798822948723
eBook ISBN: 9798822948730

Fee/MAH/Leh

I Am you

She is Her

We are one.

CONTENTS

INTRODUCTION

Approximately twenty billion or so light-years away from Earth, near the center of the universe, lies a solar system that defies our laws of physics. Some believe it to be the pinnacle of creation. The exact point where light separated from darkness and expanded throughout the cosmos. The largest and oldest galaxy in this dimension. Unmeasured by time, it was the first to take form and support various forms of life. Within this galaxy is a solar system that has nine planets and three suns, with a few artificial moons, and each of them is able to sustain life of its own. At first glance one would notice that a few of those planets are similar to Earth, the only real difference being that these planets are teeming with females of different genera.

While some were born to this unique part of the heavens, some of the inhabitants were rescued from different areas of the universe. A small number of them escaped persecution by learning of their origins and connection to an ancient stream of energy, which forged their unbreakable bond with other females.

These planets have no governments or ruling classes or hierarchies to speak of. Poverty, prejudice, and cultural conflict are unknown. The planets' natural way of life serves all inhabitants and gives them a naturally safe environment in which to thrive, and these inhabitants' scientific and technological achievements are a blessing that has benefited everyone, including the planet itself, making it a vibrant world full of life and natural wonders—a utopia for all intents and purposes.

However, it is a completely matriarchal society that no man has ever seen and lived to tell the tale. This is truly NO MAN'S LAND.

CHAPTER 1
DAY OF BIRTH

"Matching spirits"

This was sure to be an exciting day for Oriyah. This day marked her two thousandth birthday. She had come of age and was now ready to join the ranks of official matriarchs. As the daughter of one of the most recognized warriors on the planet, she had looked forward to this since she started training. Oriyah could now travel the universe and do what her mother and others before her had done: bring light to the darkest corners of the cosmos and rescue females who were forcibly controlled in male-dominated civilizations. They did this by taking it upon themselves to fight fire with all other elements combined.

In their society, not every female was a warrior, but if you chose to become a matriarch, you had to undergo intense mental, spiritual, and physical training for approximately a thousand years. Only then could you be strong enough to take on the chaos the void created, but a thousand years was a little more than a blink of an eye to the females that lived here. Time was a concept that had little to no meaning on this planet.

During training, as well when trainees personally observed missions off planet to observe their enemy, a variety of subjects were studied, including, but not limited to, combat techniques, weapons training, biology, and quantum physics, along with different varieties of science that only enhanced their ability to manipulate the energy that surrounded all things. This was a process that created the fiercest warriors, warriors who were feared by monstrous creatures that would give anyone nightmares.

They believed without any doubt that male kind came from the deepest depths of the void and was made in the image of the celestial father of chaos, created to be a more robust copy of the original form of life, as a counter to the separation of light that had resulted in the creation of the female. Their truth was that females were the light that illuminated the void. An intense connection with the natural flow of life, partnered with the ability to create life on their own, had them believe they were made in the image of light itself, the celestial mother. The one who had freed herself from darkness and given life to them all.

That being said, all the inhabitants had seen that male kind's plan was to infect nature and control all life. To shroud the light in darkness and pass itself off as authentic while raping the light of the essence and ability to shine. Male kind continued to be a plague that must be dealt with. The experienced had seen that compassion did not work. Words were unheard. Pain was ignored, and to male kind love meant obedience. Males were chaotic beings who had no sympathy for anything outside their own agenda. Male kind's reason for being was to kill, and males seemed to comprehend only pain. So a warrior that was trained to kill the killers was a miracle to the females who prayed to a man to save them from another man.

During her training she became one of the most skilled, fierce, intelligent, self-aware warriors the planet had ever seen. None of her teachers or instructors could understand where her power originated, and no amount of scientific studying could explain the phenomenon. She was without a doubt her mother's daughter.

While still asleep, she dreamt of a planet that held some resemblance to Earth. She heard a bloodcurdling scream and the sounds of a whip as people's cheers and applause reverberated in and out. At the same time, repeated strikes were felt all over her body, and with each strike she saw a different image of a badly beaten pregnant woman, the identity obscured because the face was distorted and covered in blood. Another vision showed the silhouettes of nine figures surrounded by darkness, while the last image, of a dagger in the stomach of said woman, was enough to put a sudden stop to her slumber.

Drenched in sweat and breathing heavily, she slowly caressed the scar above her heart as if she had felt the dagger in the dream pierce her chest. She was clearly irritated with a recurring dream whose meaning she had yet to understand. She flopped back down and stared at the ceiling. As the images repeated over and over in her mind, she whispered to herself, "What does it mean?" A question that directly motivated her training to become a warrior like her mother.

Moments later she got up and walked over to her bedroom window. As she gazed into the sky, out of the corner of her eye Oriyah caught a glimpse of her reflection but noticed it was not her own. However, when she looked at it directly, it was identical. She moved away slowly, feeling a little shaken, and noticed that the distance changed the way the face appeared. The revelation was seemingly always just out of reach.

She was taken aback by something that was becoming a part of reality outside dreams. Plus the fact that it was happening on her birthday, which was the same day as her official graduation. She took a deep breath, gathered her emotions, exhaled, and then opened the window. She closed her eyes as the cool breeze flowed into her room and smiled as she opened her eyes and looked upon the beautiful scenery on their planet: the sparkling light of the yellow star, the variety of creatures that soared the skies, the gorgeous mountains covered by colorful, lush vegetation, and the pristine waterfalls that flowed without end. She lingered in the moment, taking it all in, because she felt like she would not see it for a long time. Suddenly a wave of sadness overwhelmed her spirit, causing her heart to beat ten times faster than usual. She took a few more deep breaths in an attempt to calm herself, during which she heard a chirp coming from the multiuse wrist gauntlet on a chair, tucked under her hooded cloak.

Seconds later, she heard her mother's voice saying, "My precious stardust. My only child. The light that gives me life. I am so proud of you. I've heard nothing but good things. Please come and see me before the gathering for your graduation—I have something for you." The message cut off. A second later, it came back on, and her mother said, "Oh, and grab some Niribu fruit and wine on your way here...Fēmálè!"

She was overjoyed, as her mother's words brought with them a feeling of warmth and excitement. She quickly grabbed a golden disk a little larger than a quarter and placed it on the opposite side of the scar on her chest. The disk started to spread as it replicated itself to become a layer of nanites that conformed to her body.

As a mood ring changes colors based on emotion, her biosuit performed in the same manner, plus adapted to any environment. Soon after, she grabbed her customary white hooded cloak and multiuse wrist gauntlet, also known as an MUG, and stood in front of the window.

She smiled and basked in the glow of the yellow star and dove out the tenth floor of the twelve-story building while yelling with joy on the way down. She hit the ground with enough force to create a small crater and a considerable gust of wind that made a big mess.

"ORIYAH!" Yoruba yelled. Yoruba was her instructor and her mother's esteemed colleague. She was also one of the oldest females on the planet, one of the original matriarchs who had purged the planet from patriarch rule. She was known for her knowledge and brutality in battle. As she was a female who had seen and felt the pain that male kind had caused, her lack of mercy was justified.

Oriyah looked back and saw her teacher covered in dust and debris from her tricolored flower garden. "Ooops, I'm sorry," she said as she darted toward the forest, barely missing another one of Yoruba's gardens while yelling, "Fēmálè!"

As Oriyah ran across the surface of a nearby lake, barely making a ripple, Yoruba shook her head and smiled, then whispered to herself, "And I am you." She then glanced down at the small crater and noticed a flower slowly growing from the base of Oriyah's footprint. She looked on at Oriyah proudly as she watched her vanish into the forest. She felt the kind of pride a teacher feels when her student succeeds.

While speeding joyfully throughout the forest, carefully dodging trees and a diverse lot of woodland creatures, Oriyah then leapt into the air and grabbed hold of a nearby tree branch and swung from branch to branch with the agility of a lemur, enjoying every moment like a child at play. In the act of swinging, she approached the end of the forest, which gave way to a large grassy field. When she reached the last branch, she grabbed hold with both hands, then swung herself into the air and completed a quadruple backflip with a twist that would have left a lifelong gymnast in awe.

She then gazed upon the grass-covered field and suddenly took off sprinting across the field, creating small shock waves with every step. A few moments later, she clumsily tripped over her own foot, falling to the ground. She tumbled across the open field, kicking up dirt and grass. She immediately stood up and looked around to see if anyone had seen her embarrassing fall. She couldn't help but laugh at herself as she wiped away the debris from her clothing. She glanced around once more to be absolutely sure nobody saw her. Right before she took off running again, she heard a giggle from the tree line behind her.

"Who's there?" Oriyah shouted. She got no response, but she could still hear the soft, stifled giggle.

"I said, who's there?!" she shouted even louder. She then heard a loud laugh coming from behind a tree. Her longtime friend peeked her head from behind the tree and fell to the ground holding her mouth before bursting with laughter.

"Imajin!" Oriyah exclaimed in shock. "Why are you hiding?"

Still laughing, Imajin replied, "Isn't it obvious? I was waiting on you." She gasped for air and then added, "I was going to try and scare you, but that fall did enough damage. Are you okay?" she added, teasing Oriyah. "I've never seen someone fall that hard in my life!" She then stood up and walked over to Oriyah and pulled a piece of grass from her hair. "You missed a spot."

And fell back to the ground laughing.

Oriyah smiled and shook her head. "That is so wrong! And here I was thinking we were the best of friends."

"I'm sorry, my light. I just couldn't help it. I saw you laughing at yourself after you stood up. So you already know how embarrassingly funny it was. That's why you looked around to see if anyone saw you," Imajin replied. She then jogged over to where Oriyah initially fell. She looked at the ground, at the same time waving her hand around the area. "How does one trip over air?"

They both laughed. Oriyah ran over and playfully jumped on Imajin's back, causing the both of them to fall to the ground. While straddling her back, Oriyah started to tickle Imajin. "No, no, no, don't do that. I'm going to mess myself!" Imajin responded.

"Hmm, I wonder how funny that would be," Oriyah replied.

They rolled around in the grass laughing. Oriyah wrapped her legs around Imajin's waist and continued to tickle her. Imajin tried her best to get out of Oriyah's hold, to no avail.

"It's not fair," Imajin responded. "You're trained and I'm not. This is easy for you."

Oriyah said with a smirk on her face, "Yes… yes, I am."

"Please, I beg of you. I'm going to tell your mother," Imajin replied as she struggled to get free.

Oriyah suddenly stopped and said, "Why do you have to bring my mother into this?"

That moment was all Imajin needed. She turned around and grabbed Oriyah's cloak and pulled it down toward her. "Ha! I got you," said Imajin. They wrestled around playfully until they were both out of breath. They lay in the grass to catch their breath. Oriyah turned to her and said, "You called me your light."

"Did I? Hmm…I don't remember that. I did say it's bright out here. I see how you could confuse the two," Imajin replied.

Oriyah smiled and said sarcastically, "Yeah, it sure is bright. So bright it pains my eyes."

Imajin giggled, grabbed her hand, kissed it, and said, "Yes, I did say my light." Shen then added, "Is that okay?"

Oriyah smiled, then answered, "I have no issues with it."

Imajin gently caressed Oriyah's face and said, "I've waited so long to see you again. At times, I wanted to bust down the doors of the matriarchs' hive and demand that they let me see you. I've thought of nothing else but to be with you once again."

Oriyah replied bashfully, "I didn't know you felt that way about me. Just so you know, I feel the exact same way about you."

"I was hoping you'd say that," Imajin replied.

Oriyah stood up, held out her hand. "Walk with me."

Imajin smiled, grabbing her hand. "I'd be delighted. I'd follow you anywhere." Holding back laughter, she added, "As long as we're not running. I'd hate to see you fall again."

Oriyah looked at her and gestured as if she were about to tickle her again.

Imajin quickly said, "Okay, okay, okay…no more mentions of that very embarrassing tumble."

Oriyah laughed. "Thank you."

Moments later, as they walked toward town, Oriyah gently pulled her hand away from Imajin. Imajin turned and asked, "Did I do something wrong?"

"No!" Oriyah replied. "It's just that my hands are sweaty and sticky. I never thought I'd hear those words coming from you. I thought that you only saw me as a friend. I'm shocked and weirdly nervous. I'm sorry."

"You don't have to apologize," Imajin replied. She then grabbed Oriyah's hand and added, "I don't mind the sweat or the stickiness. It is you, and I adore everything about you. I can only wish to be more like you."

"More like me? What do you mean?" Oriyah asked.

"Well, you're a strong, courageous, intelligent, all-around driven female. Me, on the other hand…I'm none of that. I've tried to change, but in my mind, I'm still stuck on Ramus—my home world," Imajin answered. "When you're born a prisoner deep underground, it's hard to change."

"I've seen some footage of your world, but the information on its entire history isn't complete," Oriyah replied.

Imajin reluctantly added, "They made female-like androids to replace us, and those were programmed with an obedience code. However, when they wanted the real thing, they would come to us. I hate to remember them raping my mother in front of me. They laughed and stared at me while it happened. When finished, they strangled her for fun and left the body there for me to watch it rot. I was but a child when it happened. Like so many others on my planet." Imajin closed her eyes and said with a tremble in her voice, "The things they did to us…we were helpless. We didn't know how to fight back. We never questioned 'Why us?' because it was all we knew. We were made to believe they had created us and our purpose was to serve and comply with whatever they had in mind." Pausing briefly, she added joyfully, "Until I arrived here."

Oriyah pulled her in close and looked deeply into her eyes. "You don't have to change anything for anyone. I adore the female you were, the female you are, and the female you will become. You are perfect in every way. I cannot imagine the things you've seen and been through. You've seen the callousness of the male up close. I've only seen holographic simulations during training and observed them during training. I do know they have no pity or remorse."

She held up her fist, grinned, and continued, "And I am more than ready to seek them out and steal their life while crushing their ideas. I can't wait to begin." After kissing Imajin's cheek, she added, "You just be you, and I will take care of everything else. I will be whatever you need me to be whenever you need me to be. No male will ever harm you again." She gently moved Imajin's hair from in front of her face and then asked, "Do you understand, my light?"

With watery eyes, Imajin bashfully answered, "Yes, I understand, and thank you."

"It's the truth. You don't have to thank me," Oriyah said. "You're stronger than you know. If you stay in the dark, that means you live in the dark, and if you live in the dark, you can't see or feel the warm embrace of the light. So in other words...you have to move."

Imajin smiled. "Your mother said the same thing."

Oriyah, shocked, replied, "So you've been chatting with my mother?"

"She saved me," Imajin replied. "Without her, I wouldn't be with you right now. I'm more than grateful." She then took a moment to reminisce while looking in the sky. "I remember the ground shaking like an earthquake that wouldn't stop. It went on for days and days. When it stopped— your mother!" she exclaimed.

"One small yet very intimidating woman walked into our prison covered in blood. There were still chunks of flesh attached to one of her blades. She used our cell bars to scrape off the chunks of flesh. She was so calm. It was terrifying, but her aura or energy was warm and inviting while being relieving at the same time.

"She stood in front of us, and like something from a dream, her body, along with her blades, started to glow. The brighter she got, the more heat came from her body, to the point where the blood kind of evaporated into nothing. Afterward she gave us a choice: we could either stay shrouded in darkness or come with her and live in the light, in a place where you are in charge of your own life.

"Most of us thought she was a monster and were reluctant because of that assumption. Plus there was the fact that none of us had been above ground. All we knew was the life we were living—the darkness of the depths was our way. It was normal to us until I came here. She freed me from death and gave me the choice to live as I please and see the truth. So yes, I talk to your mother often."

Oriyah tearfully replied, "Well, I'm even more grateful because I got to meet you. I can tell you the first time I saw you. Your spirit winked at me, and your aura grabbed ahold of me before you smiled or said hello. I've cherished that moment for so long. It is something I will never forget." She held Imajin tightly in her arms and said, "All the darkness you've seen—I feel so privileged to be your light."

Imajin blushed, kissing her on the cheek. "You have darkness too."

Confused, Oriyah asked, "What do you mean?"

Imajin placed her hands gently on Oriyah's temples and replied, "Those dreams you've been having."

"How did…you know?" Oriyah said, stumbling over her words.

"I don't know," Imajin answered. "Since I've been here, when I'm close to someone or when I look into someone's eyes, I can see and feel their turmoil. I can see what keeps them from becoming their true selves. It's hard to explain."

Oriyah grinned. "And you say you wish to be more like me. That's a skill that took me years to comprehend, and to be completely honest, I still haven't mastered it." She then took a deep breath. "There is something that worries me. I have this recurring dream, but not a dream. It is like flashes of images and different sounds. I see the same six images over and over. All random, no order to them at all, and the same horrific noises. The one that gets me the most is one of a pregnant woman. Her face…it's swollen, with blood coming from her head, mouth, and her eyes. Like she's crying blood. Her body was bare, and I could see a cut across her stomach…" Oriyah paused. "It's horrible, and this morning, while I was looking out the window, My reflection kept changing between me and the female from my dreams." Oriyah stopped walking and sat down on a nearby boulder. "I don't know what it means, Imajin! What does it mean?"

Imajin kneeled in front of her. "Let's find out. Can I try something? I would like to look into your mind and see what you see."

Oriyah asked, surprised, "You can do that?"

Imajin answered, "I think so, but you will be the first person I've intentionally tried it on."

"Umm, should I be worried?" Oriyah jokingly asked.

Imajin chuckled. "A little." She then asked, "Do I have permission to look into your mind and explore your thoughts and memories?"

"Permission granted," Oriyah answered.

"Okay, give me your hands and close your eyes. Remember the visions and breathe slowly. Let me see what you see," said Imajin. Seconds later, after grabbing her hands, she immediately pulled her hands away.

"What's wrong?! Why did you suddenly pull away?!" Oriyah asked.

Imajin shakenly replied, "Suddenly? It felt like an eternity!"

"Did you see anything?" Oriyah asked, but Imajin just sat frozen, silent, with an almost horrified look on her face. "Imajin!" Oriyah shouted with concern.

"No," Imajin said shakenly, "I didn't see anything, but I felt...everything. It was a place without time in a place without light. I could hear heavy footsteps and growls or something that sounded like thunder. I was being beaten but couldn't see where it was coming from or who was doing it. I felt the pain of each blow, which was followed by the sound of a cracking whip. I also heard painful screams, laughter, and people shouting in joy. It was all so familiar."

"Familiar?" Oriyah responded. "I don't understand."

Imajin replied "Me either" before briefly pausing for a moment. "One and the same."

Oriyah added, "Meaning whatever I'm seeing is either past-life trauma, a future prediction, or…"

"The mother," Imajin added, finishing her sentence.

They sat silently for a few moments, pondering the meaning of it all.

Then Imajin said, "Maybe this is something you need to tell your mother and see what she thinks. I'm sure she is more than capable of deciphering the meaning of whatever you need."

"You're right, but I don't want to bother my mother with such a thing. I leave on the third rise of the blue star, and I'd rather spend that time with you than dwelling on a dream. So I don't know. I might tell her," Oriyah replied.

Imajin then added, "But she'll probably know. She is very intuitive."

Oriyah agreed.

Then Imajin asked, "Do you know why your mother chose not to stop? No one has maintained two thousand years of fighting because of the toll it takes on the female spirit. The males that know of her tremble at the sound of her name. She has introduced fear to creatures that didn't know the meaning of the word. The unmerciful Mayri, I heard they call her. She's done enough. Why not rest?"

Oriyah stood up. "Because too many screams of agony intentionally go unheard. Speaking of my mother…I have to go see her. Will you come with me?"

Imajin smiled. "Anywhere."

"Anywhere!?" Oriyah exclaimed questioningly. "Thank you for offering. I was going to ask, but you beat me to it."

With a confused look on her face, Imajin replied, "Huh? What do you mean? What did I offer?"

Oriyah quickened her pace with a smirk on her face.

Imajin chuckled. "Ah, you're saying I just offered to join you on your journey." She stopped abruptly and let go of Oriyah's hand. She then clutched a charm hanging from her necklace. "I will wait an eternity for you, but I'm terrified of what's out there. I love it here, and I don't want to leave. Plus, I'm not a fighter. I haven't trained like you."

Oriyah then added, "And yet you can look into my mind and see what can't be seen. I want this, but you need this. You were trapped for so long, and now you're free, but the fear that you could end up back on your home world is the lingering darkness that still controls your choices. Once the choice is yours, you will be what you're meant to become. Not what they made you. And once you are, just think about how many others you could save. The choice is yours, my light." Oriyah reached out her hand. "I would never try to take that away from you."

Imajin smiled, grabbed her hand, and continued walking.

When they reached town, they stopped and got her mother's wine and fruit. They then stood in front of her mother's high-rise complex, which was one of the tallest buildings on the planet—a building that housed newcomers and matriarchs and also provided wireless energy to all in the countryside. They stood there silently gazing into each other's eyes.

Meanwhile, some of the female inhabitant passersby watched gleefully, as their match was known throughout the town. Love's kiss seemed imminent as Imajin and Oriyah moved closer and closer toward each other. Numerous hand and cheek kisses did not prepare them for this moment.

Their lips touched while their minds melded. They embraced each other closely as their hearts started to beat in unison, as if they shared but one. In a world full of life, at that moment there were only two. They each opened their eyes at the very same moment and gazed deeply into each other's eyes, not wasting a single moment with an ill-timed blink. They shared a joyful smile that came with a sense of mutual surety that their feelings were true of one another.

Eyes still locked in, Imajin asked, "Will I see you afterward?"

"Yes," Oriyah answered. "Will you go with me to our graduation? I would like you to be there."

Imajin replied, "I can't wait." She placed her hand gently on Oriyah's cheek and gave her another kiss.

Beaming with pure joy, Oriyah watched as she walked away. Imajin glanced back and saw her still watching. Oriyah grinned from ear to ear, turned around, and jumped high into the air grabbing the ledge of one of the balconies four stories up.

A stunned Imajin shouted, "I would be worried, but at least you're not running!"

While hanging from one arm, Oriyah glared back at her with a scathing look on her face, after which Imajin sarcastically shouted, "What!? I would never knowingly tell anyone that you tripped over air and fell while running. I would never tell people to go to the field near the lake and see the Oriyah-sized crater your body made from the impact. I love you too much to do such a thing!"

Oriyah teasingly stuck out her tongue, shook her head, and continued to climb.

CHAPTER 2
ONE AND THE SAME

"I Am You"

While climbing up the side of the building for no reason whatsoever, other than impulse, after catching sight of her mother's high-rise corner apartment on the far side of the building, Oriyah maneuvered her way toward it by quickly jumping from ledge to ledge and grabbing any small crack or crevice she was able to fit her fingers into. She continued to climb higher and higher until she became a blurred sight to the passing patrons far below. Nearly near her mother's place, she stopped and took a moment to enjoy the breeze and bask in the sunlight before noticing her mother's patio window was open. Hanging on with one hand, she placed her feet on the wall, mustered some strength, and flung herself toward her mother's window. When she was a few meters away, midair, the window suddenly closed. Oriyah thought to herself, "Well, this was a dumb idea." An idea that could've put a stop to her journey before it started. She quickly reached out and managed to grab the bottom of the windowsill.

Holding on with barely any grip, she was able to pry open her mother's window and pull herself up. She peeked in and saw her mother pacing back and forth, deep in thought, before returning to the soup that was currently boiling over. She continued to shimmy her way in as her lower body dangled on the outside, all while also trying contain her laughter. "Raaaar!" she loudly growled at her mother. Mayri broke the handle from the wooden spoon she was using to stir the soup, and within a split second, she was in Oriyah's face with the sharp point near her throat. At that moment Oriyah caught a glimpse of Mayri the unmerciful, and it was a terrifying sight to behold. After realizing it was her child, Mayri quickly jumped back and said, "Don't scare me like that. I was cooking and deep in thought. I'm sorry, my stardust."

"It's okay," Oriyah replied. Then she added, "However, I didn't expect that reaction. Here I am thinking I'm scaring you, and you end up frightening me." She then added embarrassedly, "I also think I'm stuck and maybe a little afraid to come all the way in…"

Her mother sternly said, "If you don't get in here, I'm going to push you back out. We both know you're going to land on your feet."

Oriyah smiled and wiggled her way in and confidently agreed, "True."

As she climbed in and tried to get her footing, she clumsily knocked over nearly everything in sight.

Her mother looked at her, walked over and grabbed her arm to help, and jokingly asked, "Are you okay? It seems as if you may need a couple more years to learn to walk properly."

Oriyah laughed and said, "In a thousand years, someone would still need to teach me to climb through a window, but I can walk through a door just fine."

Her mother then asked, "Well, why not use the door?"

Oriyah hugged her mother. "I have no idea."

Her mother smiled and turned her attention back to the soup simmering on the stove. She then said, "Must've been hard to climb up here with my fruit and wine?"

Oriyah stood there, noticeably abashed. She shook her head. "Imajin still has them."

Before her mother could reply, they heard a knock at the door.

She opened it, and there was Imajin, holding out the wine and fruit. Oriyah reached out as Imajin playfully moved the items around so she couldn't grab them. Like a game of keep-away. Then Imajin jokingly added, "You forgot something."

Oriyah snatched the items and said, "Thank you."

They both smiled as Imajin waved at Oriyah's mother and said, "Hello, Mayri. Did you get your wine and fruit? Or did your daughter climb all the way up this building just to forget I was holding them?"

Her mother walked to the door, gave Imajin a hug, and said, "The second one. I noticed it after she climbed in the window trying to scare me." Mayri grinned, turned around, grabbed the items out of an embarrassed Oriyah's hands, and walked back to attend to her soup.

Imajin then sarcastically joked, "What kind of person would climb all the way up a building just to scare someone? Especially her own mother?"

Mayri then added, "Pure impulse with the intention of impressing someone."

Imajin grinned while looking at Oriyah and said, "Oh really!" She then added, "Well, I will leave you to it." She and Oriyah both smiled while they peered into each other's eyes as Imajin slowly closed the door. Mayri just looked on and smiled in the background at the amount of cuteness on display.

After the door closed, Oriyah stood there staring at the door as if she were waiting for Imajin to come back. She glanced back at her mother and saw her watching. She then bashfully asked, "What?"

"Nothing—you two are just too cute," her mother answered. "A unique pair whose connection will transcend love itself. When I first met her, I saw you in her future. You will bring the best out of each other."

She then turned down the burner, grabbed two bowls and glasses, and said, "And don't worry—she'll change her mind about coming with you."

Shocked, Oriyah replied, "How?"

Her mother interrupted. "A mother knows. Now come sit down and eat."

Oriyah sat at the table, sniffing the food. "Is this bonsai soup and Yoruba's sweet bread?"

"Yep. It's your two thousandth day of birth. I wanted to serve your favorite meal."

Oriyah looked at her. "Aww, Mother, thank you." She scarfed down the soup and bread like she hadn't eaten in days. In the midst of eating, she stopped and said, "This day started off weird, but it has been utterly amazing since. With me and Imajin, my favorite meal, the fact that I'm graduating and can now finally make you proud." She then took a bite of sweet bread. "This really is a special day."

Her mother then said, "Proud? I've been proud since you were in my belly, eating everything I ate and not saving any for me." She wiped away a few crumbs from Oriyah's face and added, "Each day you have life and each day I can see you, hear you, and hold you is in fact a special day to me."

Oriyah grinned with her teeth full of bread and said, "I am you."

Her mother then replied, "Fēmálè."

Then a voice whispered to her, saying, "One and the same."

At that moment, her mother then asked, "What was weird about your start?"

Oriyah gathered her thoughts and said, while still eating, "Well, I've been seeing the images in my dreams, but today they appeared when I was awake."

"Hmm, on the day of your birth. It could have some significant meaning. What were the images, and how many were there?"

Oriyah swallowed her food. "Six images altogether, with no order. Planets that almost looked similar. Nine figures standing together. Although I couldn't see their faces. It was like their light was surrounded by darkness. Another one was of a bare, badly beaten woman with a spiked crown on her head, and it looked like she was hanging with her arms extended. Like she was nailed to wooden stakes." She paused briefly as she tried to remember and added, "It then showed a cut across her stomach. The last one is always the same, though. Something like a dagger plunged into the woman's stomach. Then this morning I saw a woman covered in blood as a reflection in the window, but when I got close, it would revert back to my face." Oriyah continued, "And every morning I have that dream, the scar I have from the heart surgery when I was an infant seems to rapidly pulsate, and when that happens, my emotions become angry, sad, and happy all at the same time. It's weird." She took another bite. "Imajin told me to consult you, but—" Stopping midsentence, Oriyah glanced over at her mother and saw her trembling.

Then the soup in her mother's spoon shook and splashed around inches away from her mother's face. It was as though she froze right before taking another bite.

"Mother!" Oriyah shouted with concern.

Her mother looked at her with teary eyes. "I remember when you were a child. You loved to do two things: swim and fight. Oh! And steal some of Yoruba's sweet bread." Mayri laughed. "When you were born, you had this mean look on your face, but when you looked at me…you smiled the most beautiful, cutest smile ever. My heart melted, and at that moment my priority became clear. And that is making better personal choices and protecting you from whatever shall do you harm." Her mother finished up her soup and collected their bowls and placed them in the sink.

Oriyah wondered why her mother had changed the subject. She thought to herself, Does she know something about my dreams? What is this new energy that surrounds my mother?

Meanwhile, Mayri grabbed the bottle of wine, along with two glasses, and walked out onto the patio. She sat down at the table, poured two glasses, and then looked up. "The star shines bright today."

While taking a sip of wine, she tapped the glass table, gesturing for Oriyah to join her. Still lost in thought, Oriyah got up and joined her mother, and they both took a sip.

Then Oriyah said, "Yes, the star shines bright, Mother," agreeing with her mother's observation but confused about the shift in energy after revealing her dreams in detail.

Mayri then said, "Like you, a star struggled to survive. Not by its own choice but by the choices of the one who chooses to create. A star is light trying to expand, but the darkness around it keeps it from expanding. Like you, a star started out as a little itty-bitty speck of light and grew to become something that affects galaxies."

ONE AND THE SAME

Oriyah sat there proud but still confused. "I am my mother. My mother is me. Without you, I could never be…"

Mayri tearfully smiled. "My stardust, named after our ancestor. One of the first females on Earth." Her mother leaned back. "The battles and pain they endured at the hands of male kind cannot be measured. Just like their will!"

Before Oriyah had a chance to respond, her mother tapped her wrist gauntlet and pulled up an image of a planet. "Is this one of the planets you saw?"

Shocked, Oriyah replied, "Yes."

Her mother then showed her an image of another planet. "What about this one?"

Oriyah glared angrily at the image. "Yes."

Her mother looked at her. "This is Earth. This is where my sister and I were born and you would have been born if it weren't for my curiosity and gullibility."

Puzzled, Oriyah said, "I'm so confused. I didn't know you had sisters, nor did I know you were born on a different world."

Mayri put her head down in shame. "And for that, I apologize," she said while shaking her head. "Not telling you is not the full extent of my deceit. I personally asked Yoruba and the rest of your teachers to keep Earth and all its history, other than the males that occupy the planet, out of your academic studies. At the time, I thought I was doing it for you, but now I know…it was all for me. My last days on that planet are a terrible memory that I've intentionally tried to repress."

Shocked and even more confused, Oriyah replied, "I didn't know you had any sister connected by the same womb. Please, can you explain?"

Mayri finished off her glass of wine, looked up at the clear blue sky, and paused. Then suddenly she stood up and slowly walked over to the railing. She closed her eyes, and with her back toward Oriyah, she slowly took off her wrist gauntlet and whispered to herself, "If you stay in the dark—" While taking off her hijab, she added, "That means you live in the dark." She retracted her biosuit. "And if you live in the dark, you can never—" She relinquished her cloak and slowly finished the phrase: "Feel the warm embrace of the light."

Body now bare, her backside revealed scars along her back, buttocks, and thighs. The back of her head showed tiny cuts and patches of missing hair. Her feet, all the way up to her knees, looked as though they had been set ablaze. Her wrists and hands had horrible scarring on both sides like something hot and sharp had gone through the both of them. Her mother then very slowly turned around with her arms across her stomach. She had more tiny scars with missing patches of hair upon her head and forehead, along with long lashes across her chest and breast area. Her mother remained still as tears flowed down her face. Her arms fell to her side, divulging a scar under her navel. She then said, "I'm the one from your dreams."

A shocked and saddened Oriyah replied, "One and the same."

While caressing the scar over her heart and holding back tears, Oriyah asked one question: "What happened?"

Her mother bent down, grabbed her cloak, and put it back on. "My star, that is a story I've never told anyone, but it's time you know everything. No more secrets. You're a matriarch, and we don't deceive each other, ever! Deception is part of the game male kind likes to play, and we don't indulge ourselves in that type of behavior." Her mother poured herself another glass and sat down. She leaned back in her seat, picked up the glass, and took a sip.

Gazing upon the setting of the yellow star over the horizon while also watching the rise of the blue star that followed was a moment every inhabitant on the planet cherished. But at that moment, Oriyah could not have cared less. Her mind was focused on those horrible scars.

Mayri took another sip. "Before I tell you the story of my pain, you must know the story of my pleasure." She smiled and added, "My life was hard but was made easy by those sisters of mine."

CHAPTER 3
THOSE SISTERS OF MINE

"Unbreakable bonds"

"Lilith, Amaterasu, Yemaya, Eve, Durga, Guadalupe, Guanyin, and Sedna," Mayri said while holding her glass in the air like she was making a toast to her long-lost sisters. She took another sip and added, "My wonderful sisters, whom I love and miss with every fiber of my being." She smiled and added, "Our time together was memorable." Oriyah could clearly see the joy and repressed pain in her mother's eyes, as if the thought of her sisters brought her instant happiness with a gloomy cloud of sadness and regret that loomed over her spirit. She watched silently, making sure not to interrupt her mother's thoughts as her mother glared into the wine glass.

Suddenly, her mother said, "Three women— each had a set of triplets. Our mothers gave birth to us soon after the great war. So it was a difficult time for all females. Our mothers found a secluded place on Mount Chomolungma to have us so they could raise us in relative peace. They passed away shortly after teaching us all we needed to take care of ourselves. We were all still very young, but we were capable."

Mayri sighed sadly and continued, "They often spoke about how tired they were. Not only their bodies, but their spirits as well. I understood after they told us the stories of the battle they'd had with male kind. Thousands and thousands of years of fighting a never-ending war against different types of males, terrestrial and extraterrestrial—it had to be tiring. They made it a purpose to teach us who and what we were so we could also teach other females, because they knew that male kind's ultimate plan was control, and our history would be diluted, then ultimately nonexistent.

"All the knowledge they had gained over the years of living on Earth and Mars they taught to my sisters and me. Everything from controlling certain elements and manipulating energy to using pressure-point combat skills to take down the biggest males. They were strict, and it was a lot to learn, but my sisters made it a great experience."

She then added, "Lilith, the so-called oldest sister, always bragged about being the firstborn, even though she was literally born seconds before Eve, and because of that she was our self-anointed guardian." Mayri laughed. "If you let her tell it, she was physically the strongest of the group. However, she might be the one that deserved the title, because during a rock-throwing contest, she picked up a huge boulder and threw it like a pebble farther than the small rocks we had. She could also pound that same boulder into rubble. She was the embodiment of strength. She was defiant and stubborn but gentle and caring."

Her mother put down her glass. "We watched her battle a giant dire wolf with her bare hands, and her only injury was a bite to the forearm. She became a battle maniac after she escaped from capture by some demon named Adam. He insisted on her being his bride.

"He tried to get her to believe that a higher power told him that she was there to serve and obey him and only him. He also tried to force himself into her.

"After that, she trained herself to become a much stronger combat-ready female." While smiling, Mayri continued, "She would pick fights with giant beasts, terrifying monsters, and win without having to use our shared abilities to control our energy. She could cut down a group of males in an instant with a huge long broadsword she would carry. She was truly unmerciful to all breeds of male kind.

"The same man tried to capture Eve as well, and he failed twice." She added, "Men are relentless when they want something, and the word 'no' just enrages them. Eve was a very sweet and innocent woman who adored nature. Her capacity for love, emotion, and forbearance was something we all were attached to, especially Lilith. They had different mothers but shared a bond that was unbreakable. When she was taken, Lilith was furious. She tore through the forest and villages, leaving broken men and buildings in her wake, until she found her." Mayri paused briefly to reflect on the memory. "And when she did find him, using all her strength, she ripped him in half by his legs, and she did it slowly. Yes, it was grotesque but also satisfying because he would never be able to do it again. On our travels, we've seen the aftermath of the horrible acts male kind does to females. So when we destroy those kinds of males…it's justice."

As Oriyah sat silently, taking in all the newfound information, the images of the horrible scarring all over her mother's body continued to replay over in over in her mind. As much as she loved hearing about her mother's family, her anger wanted to know the cause of her pain.

Mayri continued to say, "Guanyin was the one who assisted us when asked. There was never a bad time to ask her to do something. She always put what she was doing on hold just to help us with whatever we needed. Her senses and sensibility were unmatched. She could smell and see at great distance. She was very good at memorizing the constellations. She memorized the terrain and knew which direction we should travel. We'd been through seemingly never-ending deserts, blinding blizzards, and harsh jungles. She never led us down the wrong path. Always out front leading while holding a long spear that was basically her third arm because she never put it down."

Her mother pointed to the encased display on the table. "You see that blade? Beautifully made, is it not?"

"Yes. I was wondering about it when I knocked it over climbing in the window," Oriyah replied. "I've never seen it before."

Her mother added, "Sedna, our other sister, made all our weapons. The weapons she constructed were virtually indestructible. She also made this cloak I have on. I could never part with either of them. So I hid them away until today."

She took another sip of wine, then said, "She was nearly murdered by a man named Anguta. During which time she lost all her fingers on her left hand. She was also the only one among us that ever killed another female."

"Why?!" Oriyah exclaimed. "We don't do that!"

"Because a child that she closely cared for was beaten, raped, and murdered at the pleasure of Anguta and his wife. So she killed them both, but she nearly lost her life in the process. Anguta was no ordinary man. He was a killer that believed he could become stronger by consuming the flesh of women, and the younger the better. However, that ended when, with her hammer, she repeatedly bashed in his head until only his shoulders were left. Afterward, she dumped the both of them into an active volcano, and his wife was still alive when it happened. I believed she deeply regretted it, because she was never the same after that."

Just before she took another sip, she burst out laughing. "Guadalupe and Yemaya, the most lovable, caring, kind, yet insufferable duo ever!" her mother exclaimed. "They literally spoke for each other. Yemaya would speak for Guadalupe and vice versa. It was so irritating, and they did it on purpose just to annoy us, but it was also funny at times. They were like a comedic duo that always kept us laughing. Pulling pranks and joking around. They always turned our sadness or anger into happiness and joy."

Oriyah chuckled. "Did they have the same mother?"

"Nope," her mother answered. "But another tight bond. They both loved the seas as well. They had the uncontrollable urge to swim whenever we were near water. They often swam with the females of the sea, mermaids. They would disappear for days at a time and come back with souvenirs for all of us. Sea shells, pearls, and such. We'd sit by a campfire, and they'd tell us tales of their adventures." Her mother smiled. "They were both so clumsy on land. Like fish out of water. Tripping over nothing and bumping into things that were quite easy to avoid. If they weren't paying attention, the tiniest blade of grass would cause them to stumble. It was so cute." Holding back tears, her mother added, "I miss them."

A rollercoaster of emotion paired with repressed memories had Mayri frozen momentarily in time. "Sounds a lot like me," Oriyah joked, breaking the silence.

Her mother wiped the lingering tear away and replied, "More than you know, my star. I see my sisters in you and Imajin."

"Imajin! What about Imajin?" Oriyah asked.

Without answering, her mother suddenly stood up and started dancing before humming a mesmerizing tune.

Her mother replied while dancing, "Durga, the demon killer. She called this dance Bharatanatyam. She used to sing to us while moving around gracefully, using elaborate hand gestures and enchanting movements. Her voice, along with her movements, would put us in a trance."

Oriyah watched as her mother joyfully twirled around on the patio. It was as if she were back with her sisters, enjoying life as they did before. As the moment flowed, specks of light started to gather and gradually to expand. A healing energy that was shrouded in pain started to engulf the entire patio.

"Mother!" Oriyah yelled with concern.

Her mother stopped abruptly as the expanding energy ceased and started to retreat back into her body. After sitting back in her chair, she said, "None of us could sleep without her soothing hum in the background."

"Demon killer," Oriyah added, changing the subject to move on from the unnerving surge of energy she'd just witnessed.

Oriyah then added, "You called her a demon killer. Why?" She leaned back in her chair.

"Other than the fact that she defeated more than all of us, it's because she killed an ancient demon named Mahishasura. He was a three-headed cosmic demon who performed his evil by shape-shifting. He led many women and children to their deaths. He was well known; even our mothers knew of his chaos. We'd heard plenty of tales of his treachery. Our mothers never caught him, nor the women before them, but with the help of Amaterasu, she found him, and the battle lasted for three days. He died cursing all women for life because he never thought a woman would be the one to defeat him. When the battle was over, she beheaded him and burned the body."

"Wow, a battle for three days!" Oriyah exclaimed.

Mayri replied, "Yeah! Durga's combat capabilities paired with Amaterasu's speed gave her the edge she needed to finish the job. So there was no reason for us to interfere, at the time.

"Amaterasu was simply amazing!" Mayri exclaimed proudly. "Highly intelligent and as fast as a blink. The fastest of us all. She used her intelligence and invented portable items to make our travels easier. Devices that could rapidly grow fruit from the ground, mobile sleds that hovered above ground, which we used to haul our gear, and a portable wall that created a nearly invisible energy force field around our campsite. She also recreated technology lost in the great war for Atlantis and Sumbala. Plus, she was the only one who could prank the comedic duo."

Mayri smiled gleefully as she remembered, "We all knew when they came back from their sea adventures they would eat and drink nonstop, and we knew that they hated anything that was bitter or spicy."

She laughed while saying, "So one day, Amaterasu made some soup and added the hottest peppers we could find. The smell was so strong. I'm shocked they didn't notice it. And she also switched their drinks with lemon and grapefruit juice. So when they went to eat the spicy soup, they realized it was spicy. They immediately grabbed something to drink. The look on their faces when they realized what going on was precious. We laughed until our stomachs hurt while they ran around chasing Amaterasu, but catching her was nearly impossible."

Oriyah laughed seemingly joyfully with her mother, but her heart raced and anger raged—the underlying tale was moot, and her patience was growing thin. Her primary concern was not her mother's sisters but the man who had caused the scars. Why speak of the joys before pain? What was the point? Seemed kind of backward.

She asked, "What about you? I see what kind of women your sisters were, but what about you, Mother?"

Mayri stopped laughing abruptly as tears started to fill her eyes and regret punched her heart. Oriyah wondered whether she had asked the wrong question or whether her tone had been without manners. So she quickly asked a forgotten question: "What were your mothers' names?"

Her mother answered slowly, "Amaterasu, Guanyin, and Durga's mother was called Manat. Sedna, Yemaya, and Lilith's mother was called Inanna. Eve, Guadalupe, and my mother were called Asherah."

After a few moments of silence, before Oriyah had a chance to ask another maybe ill-timed question, Mayri sighed and replied, "I was curious and naïve during a time when either could cause you more pain than you could possibly imagine." She turned toward Oriyah, looking deep into her eyes. "Most of us had been captured or nearly captured, but we always escaped. Our mothers warned us more times than I can count. They taught us about the world that awaited us, but I was curious about them."

"What do you mean by them?" Oriyah asked.

"Men," her mother answered. "I was observant of all things in the natural world, but men are not a part of the natural world. They are chaotic."

"I know that," Oriyah replied anxiously. "Please tell me what happened."

"I'm getting there, my star," her mother replied sternly. "It's hard. You have to understand that I've intentionally repressed these memories because every time I think of anything from that time, I can feel my scars ache as if it's happening again." She took a deep breath while clenching the glass. "And I become furious with myself beyond control." The glass cracked, and wine started to flow down her hands and wrists.

Without saying a word, Oriyah took it upon herself to grab her mother another glass. "Thank you," her mother responded as she got up and walked to the edge of the patio. She leaned back against the railing and said, "As I said before, I was curious doing a time when curiosity could get you killed." Oriyah listened as her mother opened those repressed memories of her past.

"No," Mayri added. I was going to tell you about it, but you should see it."

"See how?" Oriyah replied confusedly.

"Fēmálè, remember?" her mother replied.

"I am you. One and the same," Oriyah responded.

Moments later, while they were lying back in their chairs in the full glow of the blue star, her mother explained, "Now I'm taking you to a certain time in my life. Keep your focus. Don't veer off, or you will get lost in the story. If you do, your mind will meld within my body during that point in time and feel everything I felt." She added cautiously, "You do not want to do that!"

"Fēmálè," Oriyah repeated.

Thereafter, things went eerily silent, as if time itself stopped. They were wrapped in a mental connection that created a type of energy that resembled a puddle of clear water and engulfed their entire bodies. Seconds later, they both lay in a trance as Oriyah fell into her mother's memories.

CHAPTER 4
A STORY TOLD ONLY ONCE

"Compassion of the heart"

A little over two thousand years ago, a young Mayri was strolling through the forest, collecting roots and berries for breakfast. Something she did every morning for her sisters. However, this time she heard a whimper in the distance. Curiosity enticed her to seek out the noise, and the closer she got, the more it sounded like the pained cries of a wounded animal that came from a small cave formed into the hillside. Instinctively, she rushed to help. Upon entering, she saw what looked like a malnourished child covered in dirt, cuts, and bruises. A bone was protruding out of the child's lower leg, and it had a huge gash on the back of its head. She bent down to help until she saw it was not a child but a man.

Insight told her to walk away, but curiosity caused her to hesitate right before she made the decision to exit the cave. "Help," the man said hoarsely as he weakly crawled toward her. "Please, help me," he pleaded.

Mayri knew the history of the first women and remembered her mother's teachings. The first women helped the savage cavemen in need only to be raped and defiled for their troubles. Although there was one man who went against his nature and fought for females. He was able to get a few others to follow his lead and change their ways to live peacefully with women. It was a true era of balance and prosperity in the ancient days.

She looked into his watery eyes while contemplating the choice before her. Taking a few moments to examine his mangled body, she knew he would not survive using natural remedies. The use of her healing ability was the only way.

"No," her brain yelled. "Yes," her heart screamed even louder.

Compassion of the heart distorted the clarity of the mind and manipulated her intuition. In that moment she made her decisions. He reached out for her and fell to the ground. She walked toward him and knelt to his side and said, "I will do what I can. Just be still."

Moments later, her hand started to glow before she placed it on his forehead, after which his body slowly healed. At the same time, it was as if something dark grabbed ahold of the light within her. The more his body healed, the more the light in her dimmed. Before the process was over, she pulled back her hand, stood up, and fell against the cave wall.

The man open his eyes for a moment and asked, "Who are you?"

"Mayri Magdalene," she replied. "What is your name? Where are you from?" she added.

With a puzzled look, he replied, "I don't know," before blacking out.

Every fiber of her being told Mayri to get back to her sisters and leave the man to his own devices. Again, she went against her mother's lessons and own intuition. She sat there patiently waiting for the unknown man to regain consciousness. Now, her life and spirit had intertwined with his. Compassion of the heart distorting intuition.

An hour or so before nightfall, the man finally awakened. He looked around and saw Mayri staring at him. "What did you do to me? How did you do it?" the man asked.

"I healed you as much as I could, but I was unable to finish," Mayri replied.

"How?" he responded.

"We just can," she replied. "It's difficult to explain."

"What do you mean by…we?" he asked.

"Females…" said Mayri. "Do you remember your name or how you got here?" she added.

After taking a moment to think, he answered, "No, it's all a blur."

"It will come with time," Mayri replied. "Rest here and gather your strength. Good luck on your journey."

As she turned to exit the cave, the man pleaded, "Wait…please take me with you. Don't leave me here alone."

"I'm sorry, but I can't. My sisters don't really trust male kind," she replied.

"Why? I would never harm an innocent," the man said.

"But most of you will," Mayri replied.

"Not me…please, only for a little while. Until I'm strong enough. I won't survive without you," he added.

Mayri pondered What if? in that moment. She knew her sisters would not agree with this man living with them. But what if she could change the nature of one man? Teach him ancient knowledge, care for him, and maybe build a better future for women everywhere? Because at this point in time, being a woman meant obedience or death.

"Okay, but do not speak. Just let me do the talking, or they might kill you," Mayri added.

The man used the cave wall to stand up and said, "I won't say a word. Can you help me walk?"

She looked around and grabbed a broken branch from near the cave entrance. She handed it to him and said, "Use this to walk."

"Why can't you help me?" he replied.

Mayri sternly added, "Our flesh will never come in contact ever again." She glared into his eyes and asked, "Do you have a problem with that?"

Seeing the seriousness in her eyes, the man replied, "No…none. Your body, your choice."

"Very true. Now, follow me," Mayri added.

While they made their way back to camp, Mayri knew it would be hard to get them to go along with her plan, but she had to find a way to convince her sisters to trust in her intuition. Every single one of her sisters had suffered at the hands of men after caring for them. How was she going to dispel their doubts? It was sure to be a hard task.

The closer they got to the campsite, the more her nerves rattled. She could see them all gathered around the campfire, talking and laughing per usual. "Wait here," Mayri said to the man. "Do not approach until I tell you it safe."

He nodded in agreement and said, "Understood."

She slowly proceeded to their camp, contemplating her words, but before she could say anything, Sedna asked, "Where have you been? We were getting worried."

"Yeah, you usually don't take this long," Eve chimed in.

"Were you following insects again?" Durga joked.

As they all chuckled collectively, Yemaya and Guadalupe glanced at one another and immediately knew something was off. "What's wrong with you two?" Amaterasu asked.

"What did you do this time?" the duo asked in unison.

But before she got a chance to reply, without warning, Lilith darted toward her so fast she didn't have a chance to react. Noticing she wasn't coming for her, she turned around and saw Lilith clutching the man's throat as his legs dangled in air. He tried to free himself but couldn't get past the strength of her death grip. The man's eyes cried out, "How could a woman be this strong?" as he clawed at her hand and struggled to breathe.

A few seconds later, shortly before he blacked out, Eve struck him with a front kick, which was followed by Yemaya's straight right punch to his sternum, a blow that sent him flying backward, releasing him from Lilith's grasp. While he was still in the air, Durga's staff smacked the side of his head like a bat striking a baseball. He hit the ground, tumbled around, and landed on his back. He opened his eyes and saw Guadalupe midair with ill intent. Then she descended with a two-foot stomp to his chest. The man groaned loudly in pain as the sound of his ribs breaking reverberated in the distance. It was a devastating combination of attacks, of which Guanyin was about to deliver the final blow.

"Wait!" Mayri yelled.

Flabbergasted, they all stopped and stared at her confusedly.

After a brief moment of silence, which was interrupted by a blood-filled cough, Guanyin asked,

"What do you mean, wait?" with the point of her spear hovering a centimeter away from his eye.

Mayri stuttered and stumbled over words as she began to explain, "Mmm, I...I..."

"You invited him, didn't you?" Yemaya asked.

"Yes," she replied nervously.

After a long, tension-filled moment, Guanyin said, "You stay," referring to the broken man. "You walk," she then said to Mayri.

A few yards away from the cries and listening ears of the unknown man, they gathered in front of Mayri. "Why did you invite him here?" Amaterasu asked.

"Well, he was nearly dead?" Mayri replied.

"He didn't look nearly dead!" Durga exclaimed.

Mayri replied, "I partially healed him before you broke him again."

"WHAT!?" they shouted collectively.

"He begged me. I couldn't just leave him there to die," she replied.

"We never use our abilities to heal them. You know this!" Sedna retorted.

"You couldn't or wouldn't?" Eve asked skeptically.

"What in the name of the mother were you thinking?" Guadalupe shouted.

"Diayhd," Lilith chimed in. "That's who you were thinking about, weren't you?"

Before she had a chance to reply, Durga shouted, "That was a fluke. Just one man. You know what women have been through after trying to live peacefully with them."

"Yeah, but times change. We never really took the time to teach mankind the truth about females. We just showed them the basics," Mayri replied. "What if we did show them a different way of life? And if we did, it would create a better future for women everywhere."

"So you're willing to base your life—well, our lives—on a what if," Sedna added. "With men, the past often repeats itself. That's why their past is relevant to our future. They will only change when it's beneficial to their agenda. Teach him what we know, and he will either use it against us or use our knowledge for his own self-interest."

"How can you be so naive?" Eve chimed in.

"Men prey on the vulnerable, and a woman's compassion is seen as a weakness," Lilith added. "Are those not our mother's words from experience?"

Mayri replied, "Yes, but if there's a chance we could help make a better future, shouldn't we at least try?"

Yemaya scoffed as Guadalupe said, "You can't tame chaos."

"But what if?" Mayri replied.

Shaking her head in disappointment, Durga approached her aggressively until they were nearly nose to nose. She then said, "Keep him away from us. Don't give him any specifics into who we are or our past. Say nothing about our abilities or where we've been or where we're going."

"Then I wouldn't be able to tell him much," Mayri replied.

"You'll figure it out," Durga responded.

Guanyin dropped her spear and wrapped her arms around Mayri and said, "My dear sister, I know your intentions are pure. I just hope this doesn't backfire on all of us."

After which they all turned their backs and walked away, leaving her to care for the unknown man alone.

Throughout the year, until summer came back around, the still unknown man traveled with the sisters and followed Mayri during her everyday life. During that time, he was very polite and re-spectful of their space, a seemingly good man with no bad intentions. Over time, they started to become more comfortable with him, and the more comfort they felt, the more the sisters opened up.

They taught him things to help him survive, like how to use the stars to navigate at night, how to use natural remedies and medicine. How to make bread to fill up when food was scarce. They also provided him with adequate clothing and a decent weapon for his journey. In the winter they all slept in the same shelter for warmth. He be-came a friend, a sibling, a member of their family. They developed an unwavering trust in the man they now called brother.

Before long, they all started to reveal more about themselves. Where they were born. Their mothers and the women before them. Also, the ce-lestial mother. The great war of genders that had spread across the cosmos, and the ancient stream of energy that connected all life. Plus the fact that, depending on how in tune they were with nature and their own spirituality, women could tap into that stream of energy and use it in multiple ways, including the elements. They could also use it to heal life-ending wounds.

However, when they told him that men could also tap into a certain energy and use it to become pawns for a darkness that fed on the chaos they would cause, you could clearly see the skepticism in his face, but he listened, learned, and would reply with intellect in order to understand more. As more time passed, the sisters now collectively thought that maybe he could be the one to teach male kind a different way so they could all live peacefully together in spiritual harmony.

A couple of months later, in the middle of summer, the sisters were taking a much-needed dip in a lake near their camp—a few hours of cooling off mixed with a bit of splashing around. Mayri was the last to leave. As she floated on her back, gazing up at the blue sky in complete bliss, intuition told her something was off. After looking around she saw the man she now called brother standing on the shore, staring at her naked body. Without moving she just stared back at him. He ogled her breasts with a distasteful grin before taking off his clothing and walking into the lake toward her.

She thought to herself, "Just another man, after all."

Now he was standing a foot or so away from her. She said to him in a seductive tone, "Do you want me?"

"Yes," he replied.

"To have me? To be yours only?" she added.

"Yes," he said with joy.

Mayri smiled and said "Not a chance" and proceeded to walk toward the shore.

Suddenly he grabbed her arm and said, "You say those things and then turn me away?"

"I will never be owned by any man," she replied. "I think it's time for you to leave."

The once polite, respectful man had revealed himself to be no different from the others.

He aggressively yanked on her arm and replied, "I have been nothing but patient and respectful."

She cracked a smile and said, "You're no different at all."

He pulled harder and added, "I deserve this. I deserve you. I've listened to your idiotic stories about creation. Your so-called connection to nature and each other. For what? Nothing?! No, you will be mine."

Mayri just kept smiling as he rambled on. He stopped speaking abruptly and yelled, "Stop smiling."

She paused briefly and said, "You're right… you deserve this."

All of a sudden, the lake started to rumble and vibrate. "What's happening?" he yelled fearfully.

"Water is not my element, but it's all energy," Mayri replied.

After that, the entire lake became eerily motionless. He released her arm and started slowly backing away until the water itself became like ice only around him. He then screamed in agony as ice started slowly crushing his legs. Seconds later, a small wave unexpectedly and violently pushed him back to the shore. Unable to move now due to his broken legs, he lay helplessly on the beach. His pain was ignored when he watched in shock as Mayri levitated and started to walk across the lake as if it were the ground itself, barely making a ripple with each step.

He frantically tried crawling away in a panicked, desperate attempt to flee. Within a split second, Mayri grasped his shattered ankle and soared nearly twenty feet in the air.

"Hoooooow?" he shouted as they ascended. "What are you?"

"We are authentic," she replied while he dangled in the air.

"I'm sorry. I will leave. Please don't hurt me anymore."

Without warning, she let go and watched as his body struck the ground below.

She started to slowly descend while watching the blood flow from his broken body.

"I gave you the benefit of the doubt," she said. "I was hoping you were different. That you could be the one, but you're all the same."

She then threw on her cloak and walked away, leaving him to bleed out and die alone. Giving the animals and insects a small feast. Circle of life, some would say.

CHAPTER 5
CONTINUED...

"Past felt presently"

A couple years later, the sisters were doing what they always did. Traveling the world, teaching, learning, caring, and fighting wherever the fight was needed. As the season reached the spring solstice, representing new life or rebirth, during that time, each of the sisters was blessed with a child growing within. The celestial mother, combined with their own spiritual growth, had enabled them to create life. However, a very not-ready Lilith and Sedna were more frightened than excited to see their swollen bellies. So they all figured it was time to go back to their birth home, Eden. To give birth to their children in a safe location.

After they had found out they were pregnant, the next morning, before they started the long trek back home, Mayri took it upon herself to wake up a bit earlier than usual so she could forage for chamomile plants to make tea in order to calm her sisters' anxiety. While searching, she came upon a necklace with a small pendant attached, with the words "the son" inscribed on the front.

As she examined the item, the crunching sound of dead leaves caught her attention. A slight feeling of trouble flowed through her body. So she unsheathed her blades and stood firm. Suddenly, the man she had once called brother appeared from the brush.

"You're alive," she said, shocked. "So I'm guessing you're here to retaliate? As your kind often does when their manhood is hurt."

"Something like that," he replied nonchalantly.

His tone and posture were those of a man who was no longer afraid of her abilities. However, that was not her worry. It was the fact that she was now with child. So the desire to fight was overwhelmed by the notion of fleeing for the safety of her unborn child.

With a devious smile, he said, "You got here earlier than usual. You almost caught us off guard."

"Us?" she replied before an arrow unexpectedly pierced the back of her thigh. While she was screaming in pain, a huge, brawny man nearly eight feet tall bashed her over the head with his fist. She fell to the ground hard but was not yet unconscious.

In a dim-witted tone, the giant muttered, "Goliath too strong for little woman." He chuckled and added, "You said this would be hard," referring to the still nameless man.

"Jacob, Abraham…Hurry and tie her up before her sisters show up. We would need an army to defeat them all."

"What about the one you promised me—Asherah?" a man named Muhammad asked.

"I told you Asherah was one of their mothers," he replied.

Muhammad then said, "Well, what about the strong one…Lilith? I want to break her."

"No!" he exclaimed. "Now do as I say and help them tie her up."

After hearing that, Mayri looked around and saw twelve men, not including the man she had called brother. As Goliath approached her with chains, without warning she plunged her blade through his breastplate into his sternum. With the blade still embedded, she sliced all the way down to his groin, subsequently ripping out his manhood. His screams were louder than her own.

They looked shocked as she stood tall, with his privates still clinging to her blade. With the blood pouring from her head and thigh, she snapped the arrow, leaving the tip inside her leg.

She glared at his disciples, and without further hesitation, Mayri went to work, using a combination of speed, precision, and her ability to manipulate energy. She defeated all but four of her foes, leaving decapitated limbs and entrails all over the forest floor until her mind and body started to wane. Feeling like she was close to collapsing, Mayri turned her attention to the cause of her misfortune. Peering into his eyes, she dashed at him with incredible speed, but mid-stride she became dizzy and weak. Then she fell over, falling face first to the ground. While she was trying to pick herself up, the nameless man made his way toward her with a confident grin and said "You're mine now" as she blacked out.

***

She awoke in a cell with her hands and feet shackled together. Dried blood blurred her vision while she looked around the dark, dreary cell. She then saw two women chained by their necks to the wall. "Where am I?" Mayri asked. However, the women remained silent.

"Where am I?" she repeated.

"Quiet," one woman whispered. "Just do as he says, and all will be well."

"Who?" Mayri replied.

Seconds later, the cell door opened, and the unknown man walked in. "You!" Mayri exclaimed.

"Yes…me," he replied with smile. Next, he raised his arm, and the women got on their knees and placed kisses on his hand. "Yeshua the Christ. Please forgive us for our transgressions," said one of the women, while the other added, "You are the son of God…the father. Women shall be silent and submit to their husbands. For the head of every man is Christ, and the head of the woman is man. And the head of Christ is God. We shall obey the will of the father and commit our spirits to him only."

While mockingly looking at Mayri, he reveled in his accomplishment and said, "And what is thy father's will?"

"To teach all women the right way to live, not to be slanderers or addicted to our temptations. For women to teach what is good. To be self-controlled and pure, to be busy at home and kind. To be subjects to our husbands, so that no one will malign the word of God."

He smiled at the both of them and said, "This is a time of fulfillment. Repent of your sins and turn to God, for the kingdom of heaven is near."

He turned to the guards and added, "Get them out of here. Give them food and shelter, for they are no longer unclean."

As the guards unchained the two women, Mayri said, "You actually believe him?"

"He is the son of the father. We are all one," they replied.

"You've relinquished your souls to a man you don't even know," Mayri shouted. "We are not servants. You do have a choice! Look within—acknowledge your mothers. The father is chaos." They both scoffed and continued to walk out as if her very words meant nothing to them. The ramblings of a heretic.

Meanwhile, now standing over her shackled body, the man now known as Yeshua said, "They will believe whatever I tell them." He then spat on a piece of cloth and proceeded to wipe the dried blood off her face and added, "All it took was a few years of traveling from one town and village to another, proclaiming the good news of the kingdom of God. I convinced people that all women were with evil spirits and disease. That these had to be burned out in order to cleanse their spirits."

"You got me to believe you were good. So I can see how they could believe your lies," she replied.

"You made it possible," he said.

"What do you mean?" Mayri asked.

He then explained, "At first, I didn't believe you until the day you killed me."

"You look alive to me," she added.

"The father…the creator of man brought me back to do his bidding. At that time, I realized I am him. He is me. We desire the same thing. Control over all life. To be revered and worshipped. Power, for all intents and purposes." He replied, "I want what I want, and I get what I want." Yeshua knelt down and added, while glaring at her pregnant stomach, "Now what is the name of the man who gave you a child?"

Mayri laughed out loud and said, "You obviously didn't listen to everything. I am authentic. I do not need man to have a child. None of us really do. You are nothing."

"Abomination," he replied, and in a spat of anger he reached down and grabbed the arrow still stuck in her leg and started to twist. As she cried out, he said "I can give you pleasure or pain" before aggressively yanking on the arrow, pulling it out. The barbs on the arrow still had some of her skin and muscle wrapped around them.

The sudden pain turned to anger, and she broke her hand restraints before clawing him across the face. Within seconds, soldiers rushed to his aid. Some violently kicked and punched her as some beat her with wooden clubs. After they stopped, Yeshua spat on her beaten body and said "You pay for this, wench" before one of the soldiers delivered the final blow, knocking her unconscious.

An hour or so later, the soldier carried her to the center of a packed town square in the city of Jerusalem. As they marched her through the streets, the attending patrons yelled obscene things while making vile gestures, spitting, and throwing rotten foods. She had no idea why people she didn't know would treat her in such a way. The only conclusion was Yeshua, and these were his followers. Then they proceeded to tie her hands to a wooden post, after which one of the soldiers looked at her menacingly and smiled while holding on to a long whip. He then aggressively grabbed her jaw and said, "Repent, witch."

"I will never bend to chaos. I will never break," Mayri said with confidence.

"You will," he replied before slapping her across the face and walking behind her.

Moments later, Yeshua said to the crowd, "Come to me, and I will give you rest. Come to me, all who are weary or burdened, and I will give you rest." He then continued, "This woman is unclean. She has lain with demons, chooses not to repent, and continues to practice witchcraft while praying to and worshipping a false god."

"The mother doesn't require prayer, nor does she want to be worshipped," Mayri shouted.

"Silence, harlot!" Yeshua yelled, as Mayri continued to say, "Only a man would desire such a thing." Then suddenly, the cracking of a whip, followed by her screams, resonated throughout the town square. The initial strike ripped open her back, exposing the muscle tissue below. Meanwhile, the crowd cheered at the atrocities on display. She tried to find some strength to fight, but the intensity of the next strike put a stop to her attempts. The following blow separated flesh from bone for her troubles.

Her screams continued as the attendees applauded the despicable act of the man they all worshipped. They did his bidding on his word alone and without question. A sense of pride, motivated by righteousness, made the brutality of their acts much more hypocritical. The overwhelming pain caused Mayri to faint momentarily, but she was immediately awakened by the next lash. She looked toward some of the women in attendance and pleaded, "Help me, please."

They smiled and laughed at her without compassion. Now she could see that some women were in agreement with her present situation. Their hearts and spirits were no longer their own because they had given away their free will.

Twelve lashes later, her body went completely limp. The next three met an unconscious woman with no knowledge of her current situation. While in a dream state, she saw her sisters all sitting around the campfire, watching and listening to Durga sing and dance. She thought of Yemaya and Guadalupe's pranks as they all keeled over laughing, their travels and the places they'd been. In that moment, she was alive without pain, all of them doing what they loved. She envisioned a happy life for her child, who flourished to become a formidable woman. The vision was real in her eyes, but what was actually happening was not. The future of her and the child was bleak.

Mayri awoke in a daze, in a pool of her own blood. The lashes covered not only her back but her buttocks and legs as well. Then she saw Yeshua hovering over her. He said, "You did this to yourself. All you need to do is serve me, give yourself to me, and I will stop this." She laughed and coughed blood simultaneously. He sighed in frustration and said, "You know, when I would see you and your sister interact with people, I saw that all people want someone to follow, someone to make choices for them. They want to be controlled. All of you could've capitalized on that want, but you choose to be nothing." He continued, "They will believe anything as long as it's creative. While you were teaching me, I was studying you."

"I should've left you in that cave," she replied.

"But you didn't, and now you're here," he added. He chuckled and said, "You haven't notice how weak you are?"

"What?" Mayri replied.

"That arrow that pierced your leg was covered by the same potion you gave me so I could rest. I just added a bit more ingredients to make it more potent," he added.

After a few seconds of regret in her actions, she said, "What do you want?"

"I told you: submit yourself to me. Think of your child. If you die, the child dies."

She looked into his eyes and said with pride, "No! My child will not be someone you teach your ignorant ways."

With a smirk, he replied "You brought this on yourself" as he walked out of the cell.

After he exited, a few soldiers came in to drag her weakened body to a place called Golgotha, which locals called "the place of the skulls."

Thinking she was about to be flogged once more, Mayri tried to muster up a bit of strength to fight. However strong her spirit remained, she couldn't do much with her broken body. Part of her wished her sisters would arrive to save her from this torture, but she did not want this to become their fate.

As they approached the temple, she saw a lowercase-t-shaped slab of wood with three men standing around holding onto long metal spikes and hammers. Suddenly, the overwhelming need to flee took over her mind. She fought as much as she could, but the toxins from the arrow mixed with nearly twenty bloody lashes and a broken body, followed by a few strikes to the back of the head, halted her attempts.

In dreamland once more, only this time there was no happy place. She was in a place of complete darkness, with bloodcurdling screams and demonic growls reverberating throughout the void. What is this place? She said to herself. Then all of a sudden, a bright light appeared and said in a calming, soothing voice, "Come to me."

As she approached, another voice said, "No!" but she kept on going. When she reached the light, it revealed itself to be a trap. Something demonic from within the light reached out and grabbed ahold of her.

Then suddenly she felt a hot, searing pain in her left hand that woke her up from her slumber. She was laid flat on her back on the same t-shaped wooden slab while his disciples held her down. Mayri was in shock at the sight of the long nail plunged through her hand and the burned, cauterized flesh that surrounded it. A nail that was still red from the fires they'd kept it in.

Without warning, and while she was still in shock, a second nail tore through her right hand. The excruciating pain made her forget about the first. Her cries only made the crowd cheer louder as the soldiers proceeded to force a nail through each of her feet, breaking her ankles in the process.

Before hoisting her up, they tightly tied her arms and legs down, making it nearly impossible to fall. Afterward, Yeshua was handed a black iron crown with small spikes covering the inside and the words repent & worship carved on the outside. He gracefully walked up to a dying Mayri and placed the crown on her head. As the blood flowed down her face, they started to raise her up. Even with the ropes that bound her, the weight of her own body caused the nails to tear into her singed flesh.

With pain at its peak, she could no longer cry out. The only tear shed was for her unborn child. A child that would never see the light of day, experience life, or see the beauty of nature. And she blamed herself for her fate. Compassion of the heart had distorted her intuition, and now her child paid the price. Her sisters were, in fact, right. You could be kind and love and care for male kind, but they would always be chaotic. It was their nature.

Thinking the torture was finally over, she closed her eyes and drowned out all the noise and ignored the intense pain. *I'm sorry, my child,* She whispered to herself. *Mother, into your hands I commit my spirit.* Moments later, a stabbing pain brought her out of her trance. She looked down and saw Yeshua grinning as he held the blade that pierced her below the navel. A blade that was her own.

"Death to your abomination," he said as he forced it inward a little farther, making sure to kill the child within.

Her scream created shock waves that tore through the city, silencing the crowd. The once clear blue sky instantly turned gray. Every bit of liquid in the vicinity instantly flowed red like blood. Seconds later, the grounds shook as rain, hail, and lighting pummeled the area. Then a voice called out seemingly coming from everywhere and said, *"She will not forgive. She does not forget."* Soon after, swarms of locusts appeared from all directions, ravaging the area.

Minutes later, the apocalyptic event was over. The skies were clear; the ground shook no more. The water flowed naturally, and all was calm. But the body of Mayri Magdalene was nowhere to be found. Only a bloody wooden post with the word "REMEMBER" carved into its surface.

CHAPTER 6
A MOTHER'S LESSON

"She could not forget"

After waking up from the experience of sharing her mother's memory, Oriyah remained silent for a few moments as an influx of emotions coursed through her entire body.

"You veered off, didn't you?" Mayri asked. Frozen silent, Oriyah just lay there completely still while peering into the sky. Not only was she fighting tears, but now the urge to destroy an entire planet lived within her spirit. Chaos had indeed infected her intuition.

Mayri stood up, walked to the railing, and looked at the women walking below. "Come here, my star. I want to ask you something." Oriyah reluctantly stood up and joined her mother. Seconds later Mayri said to Oriyah, "Can you see the faces of those females walking by?"

"Yes," Oriyah replied.

Her mother then asked, "What do you see? Can you see their auras?"

Oriyah took a moment to examine the females below while trying to understand what her mother wanted her to see, but the only thing she saw was the face of the man who had caused her mother pain, the women who had cheered and praised him. Which was synced with the agony of each strike that currently affected her own body, mind, and spirit.

She tried her best, but the rage inside was starting to boil over. "Yes, but I don't see or sense anything dark or chaotic. I just see me," Oriyah answered.

Mayri grinned. "That's my point, stardust. There is nothing to see, nothing abnormal to notice. These women come from all over the universe, and they know who they are and where they came from. And I'm not talking about what planets they're from. I'm referring to who created us and what we are to the universe."

She then added, "The women on Earth have no idea just how special they are. Their minds are controlled by beliefs, the color of their skin and the look of their faces and bodies. Their culture and beliefs revolve around men. Since before my time, men have been trying to implement their own design upon the world, and they did."

While looking into the horizon, her mother said, "Before my ten thousandth year, we traveled the length of the world in all directions. Guanyin wanted to map all parts of the lands we traveled. She would do the drawing, and Sedna would write the details." As she walked back to grab her glass, she added, "During that time, we helped and rescued women from all sorts of male deviance, and not just human males—other worlds' males as well. There was a time when women wanted help. Then the time came when they didn't want help. They started to submit, not only their hearts and bodies but their spirits as well."

"However, it's not their fault. Just as in other worlds, most women wouldn't be the way they are if it weren't for some man abusing them mentally or physically in their past. On Earth, fathers would sell their daughters or arrange for them to marry a man, no matter the age difference. Women and little girls were sold as sex slaves, but some of the adult women sold their bodies willingly and called it progress. Mothers would neglect their daughters while praising their sons and at the same time teach their daughters to become subservient to men. Because that was what they'd been taught to believe."

Mayri added, "Things were so unnatural they unknowingly disconnected themselves from the celestial mother. So they can no longer see themselves as the embodiment of light and life."

She continued, "Through the years, we did help some women overcome. Some became empresses, pharaohs, and queens of their countries without being married or promised to some man. Although some of them did succumb to wanting a man in their lives, and when that happened, their reigns ended.

"Just to name a few, Cleopatra, Hatshepsut, Sobekneferu, Nefertiti, and the first Sumerian queen, Kubaba, were some of the women we helped. Cleopatra was one of the most disappointing. It was very difficult making her the pharaoh after Hatshepsut, but we did, and then she joined some Roman man, and everything changed. Things become so unnatural and corrupt she took her own life. So did Nefertiti—she was hurt by the loss of her daughter, and her husband banished her because she dropped their ideal belief and reconnected with the celestial mother. He didn't want to lose control of the power he'd amassed."

She continued, "Sobekneferu wanted to look more masculine to appease or be accepted as a man by the men. That was disappointing as well.

"Now, Kubaba," her mother exclaimed, "was everything we hoped for! She was strong, fierce, influential, and intelligent, with a mind for war along with a heart for life. She reigned for one hundred years, and the women lived in peace while everyone prospered equally."

"How did you help these women succeed?" Oriyah asked, while thinking to herself,

"What's the point?"

Mayri answered with intensity, "We fought fire with fire and killed the corruption and ideals they imposed. She then explained, "Men fight other men to gain power, but women are their common enemy. An enemy whom they can never let become more influential than they are."

She added, "The point I'm trying to reach is that the chaos of men is based on a superiority complex that all of them seem to have. They see women as servants or playthings! They revel and glorify in the pain they cause others. They praise the ignitor…the flame, and they care not for the things that are burned. In their minds the things that are destroyed deserved it."

She said sternly, "If a man wants something bad enough, he will deceive, torture, or simply kill anyone in his way. They're beasts...and the beast maims when it wants something.

"Male kind was created with holes in their hearts that nothing will ever fill. They only understand power, and the ones without power often turn to their families and enact their control over them. They have primitive minds with no sense of intuition. Logic is something they do not comprehend unless it benefits their ideals. They were created as our opposite. To combat or control what we are. A more robust copy of an idea that chaos could not comprehend."

"I know, Mother," Oriyah replied, emotionless.

Mayri grabbed Oriyah's jaw, maneuvered it toward her, and looked into her eyes and said, "Chaos is not inept; it learns and evolves. Never try to change the minds of men. Even if they agree with you, they would do it only to deceive you into believing what they want you to believe, so that you can do what they want you to do. A man with power will prey on the weak. The weakest males prey upon only females and children. You cannot reason with someone who sees you as an inferior form of life."

"I understand," said Oriyah.

"Do you?" her mother asked with seriousness in her eyes.

"Yes," Oriyah answered with a persuading grin.

Mayri nodded skeptically and added, "If a man does know who he is, he will try to alter your perception of what he is. Even if he knows…don't trust him. And knowing that…don't blame the women of Earth for their ways."

Oriyah paused and looked down at the women on the street once more as her mother's words flowed through her mind, which was still partially distorted by the memory of her mother's torture. She clutched the railing, denting it with her grip, and angrily said, "But they watched and cheered as you were tortured. They threw stones and glorified participating. How can I turn a blind eye to such a thing?"

Mayri sighed lightly and placed her hand on her shoulder and said, "I know you're angry and probably want to go to Earth and avenge me, but those women don't deserve punishment; it's all they know. Not to mention—what do you think would have happened to the women if they had helped?

"I'm glad my sisters didn't find me. What if they had been captured like me?" Mayri then exclaimed, "No woman should have to experience what I went through...ever."

Soon after, Mayri walked to her room and came back holding the black thorny crown that had been placed upon her head and the blade that had been plunged into her stomach. The same objects used when she was crucified.

She then said proudly, "I think I get it now, the reason I still cannot heal myself to this day. The chaos of man is like a disease, and our light is the cure. Only we can heal ourselves by being what we are and not letting men hold sway over our future. Even though I repressed these memories, they still altered my fate because I was making decisions based on my personal past and not intuition. For a little over two thousand years, I've let chaos distort my intuition."

Her mother stood there smiling while looking down at the objects she was holding, "These things that mean absolutely nothing kept me from healing. Being strong is not enough, and being angry is too much, but a clear mind and heeding our own intuition are what helps connect us females to the elemental mother."

Oriyah watched as her mother smiled gleefully, as if she'd just had an epiphany.

"No more," Mayri whispered.

Moments later, her mother's hands were engulfed in multicolored flames. Oriyah gasped in surprise as the objects melted and disintegrated into nothing. Meanwhile, missing patches of hair started rapidly growing back upon her mother's head. The scars that covered her body vanished, along with the stab wound under her navel. The rage that plagued her emotions became serene. The chaos that diseased her spirit had been purged; now the celestial mother resided in her heart once again. At the beginning of this moment, her mother's eyes had not matched her inviting energy and smile, but now they were identical.

Mayri gazed at the fire that engulfed her hands, smiled, and said, "I haven't been able to do this in a little over two millennia."

Oriyah was happy for her mother but couldn't calm the rage that burned within her own heart.

"The man who hurt you. What was his name again?" Oriyah asked.

As the flames dissipated, her mother answered, "None of their names matter. There's nothing you can do to him or the men who helped him. We live longer than males. So I know they're long gone."

"You thought that before, and he was alive," Oriyah replied.

Changing the subject, Mayri asked, "Can I give you some advice, my star?"

"Of course," Oriyah answered.

Mayri then said, "Save the women who want to be saved. Teach them if they want to be taught. Don't try and force them to believe your words. They all have the freedom to make their own choices…so let them choose."

Mayri added, "I know you're going to Earth, and the males on that planet have been brutish and callous since the days of the first women." She then added, "Nearly a million years ago, my great-grand matriarch, Oriyah, the woman I named you after, and her counterpart, Diayhd, killed off five different species of males, and yet the human male still remains. Earth was supposed to be like this planet, but the males from other worlds placed

their experiments there to plague a once enchanting sanctuary of a planet. Their chaos plagued every form of life that called it home. Killing them is
not enough. You also have to kill their ideas, and
doing that is impossible. We've tried."

"I understand, Mother," Oriyah replied.

"I hope you do, my stardust."

Oriyah then added, "I didn't know I was named
after your great-grand matriarch. I remember you
saying that earlier when you were talking about
your sister. Thank you for that honor."

"The honor was all mine. I know what you will
become," Mayri replied.

Although Oriyah told her mother she understood, she could not forget any detail as the story
continually replayed in her mind. Her mother's
pain drowned out any words of wisdom coming
from her mother. Angry and anxious, she was
ready to leave as soon as possible. She had no
intention to waste any more energy on words.
She just wanted to instill some of what they only
seemed to understand—pain.

As it was starting to become difficult to hide
her anger, she wasted no time and said, "Well, I
have to go see Imajin. I will see you at the matri-

archs' ball." She embraced her mother and held on tight. Before she was about to leave, they heard a knock at the door. Her mother went to answer, and it was her partner, Melvenia.

"Hi!" said Melvenia. She looked at Mayri. Shocked, she added, "I've never seen you without your hijab. Why now?"

Mayri smiled and replied, "I will tell you later."

While embracing Oriyah, Melvenia asked, "Are you ready?"

Oriyah smiled and said, "Yes, I was on my way to prepare."

Melvenia then added, "Well, your ship is ready. Modified to your own specifications, complete with everything you will need to complete the matriarchs' mission. Food, water, dining area, medical bay, defense capabilities, armory, and artificially intelligent holographic computer interface. We also built a training center complete with three-dimensional holographic simulations. We basically gave you what your mother likes to have aboard her ship. You are your mother's daughter. Oh, and that idea to infuse the building material with nanites was genius. It gave the entire structure limitless possibilities of self-repair."

"Thank you," Oriyah replied. She added as she walked toward the door, "Well, I will see you later on."

"Not the window this time?" her mother jokingly asked.

She chuckled lightly. "No, I'm going to take the long way down." Before she shut the door, her mother grabbed her hand. "Remember, my star. Don't let my past pain become your anger."

Oriyah smiled convincingly. "I remember. Fēmálè."

"I am you," her mother replied with a smile.

Oriyah shut the door and whispered to herself, as she caressed the scar still above her heart, "Too late, Mother…too late."

She walked back home in a daze, not paying attention to anything except the memory itself. She felt every ounce of pain as if it were her own. Even though the scars had healed, she could still see and feel every one of them. She knew in herself she would make someone pay for what happened to her mother. A part of her wanted to destroy the entire planet. From her perspective, it seemed to be a haven for all kinds of males, and the women there were part of the problem. They either saw it

and didn't care or were too frightened to do anything about it.

Whatever it might be, she knew that without a
doubt she would find out, and she would not forget
the pain her mother had endured. Forgiveness was
not a word that resided in her vocabulary when it
came to man.

CHAPTER 7
SHE WILL NOT FORGIVE

"Lesson learned?"

A mile or so away from her mother's loft, while she was walking back to her home, Oriyah's mind continued to rage on. She stopped at a nearby lake and peered into her reflection in the water. Again, she saw the same image from before, but this time, the face was clear as day, and it was that of her mother.

Tears rapidly filled her eyes as the memory started to enrage her even more. The winds picked up speed, and the sky turned gray as the ground underneath her feet started to tremble lightly. Suddenly, a red, ominous energy started to gather, and it slowly engulfed her body. Before the energy had a chance to overwhelm her completely, she closed her eyes, took a deep breath, and slowly exhaled in an attempt to calm the anger within, but the fury wouldn't stop. She knew the men who had committed those atrocities were long gone, but she had to be sure. Even if they were gone, someone should pay.

She calmed herself, bringing back blue skies and steady winds. Moments later, after taking control of her rage, she continued to walk home.

As she approached her building, she noticed the mess she had made from leaping out the bedroom window had been cleaned. Knowing Yoruba most likely would have made her clean it herself, she looked around, but she was nowhere to be found. When she finally reached her room, she opened the door, and Imajin was standing there waiting for her. Her face lit up with joy, as the rage had momentarily disappeared.

"My light," Imajin said cheerfully.

"My love," Oriyah bashfully responded as she briskly walked to embrace her. She held her tight. "I'm so happy you're here."

Imajin replied gleefully, "You didn't think I'd be here. That's why I'm here."

Oriyah laughed and said, "That's so confusing."

Imajin smiled. "Just doing my job. Was that you earlier?"

"What do you mean?" Oriyah replied.

"That surge of energy a short while ago. It felt chaotic," said Imajin. "I've never felt that kind of energy here."

"No. That wasn't me," Oriyah replied as she took off her cloak.

FĒMÁLÈ

Imajin skeptically replied after a moment of awkward silence, "Okay, how was your mother?"

"She's doing great, now," Oriyah replied with a smile but sad eyes.

"Now? What do you mean?" Imajin asked.

"Please don't make me talk about it right now. I just want to relax for a moment. I feel so drained," Oriyah replied. She then asked, "Will you lie with me?"

"Yes, and of course I will hold you," Imajin replied as she lay down next to her.

Oriyah responded, "Good, I didn't have to ask. You're getting good at reading energy, aren't you?"

"Yep! I'm pretty good," Imajin replied with a smile.

"No lack of confidence, I see," said Oriyah as she snuggled with Imajin. They both lay silent, enjoying the time they had together. She said, "Say something, please. Your voice soothes me."

"What do you want me to say?" Imajin asked.

"Anything, whatever's on your mind or in your heart," Oriyah replied.

"In my mind or my heart," Imajin repeated to herself. She then said…

"In my mind it waits.

In the day it wakes.

In my heart it feels.

In my lungs it breathes.

On my chest, it lies.

When I'm in pain, it soothes me.

When I'm alone, it holds me.

The idea of it controls me.

It knows me—the only time I'm happy is when it takes hold of me.

I will wait a thousand years

While shedding a river of tears

To see the light looking back at me.

It makes me weak but oh so strong.

Nobody can tell me what I feel is wrong.

Being in love is what I sought.

Transcendence is what I caught.

And without looking my spirit found you.

That is my truth

That is love."

"That was…moving. You captured the words that perfectly describe my feeling for you," said Oriyah.

"Umm…excuse you, but that was how I feel about you. It was actually the first poem I wrote after I met you," Imajin replied, pleased with herself.

"Well, it's mine now," Oriyah jokingly replied.

Imajin giggled. "It's all yours, my light." She gently caressed Oriyah's head and face. "Just as I'm all yours."

Oriyah looked into her eyes. "And I'm yours."

"Fēmálè." They said in unison.

"Wait a second," Imajin replied. She gazed into Oriyah's eyes as if she were looking into her soul. "You are not planning on attending the matriarchs' gathering, are you?"

Oriyah quickly looked away.

"Look at me," Imajin said in an assertive tone.

Oriyah turned her eyes back upon Imajin.

Imajin then added while staring intently, "You plan to leave soon?"

"No, and yes," Oriyah replied.

"And that surge of chaotic energy I felt?" Imajin asked.

Oriyah answered, "That was me."

"And those images you've seen—they are connected to your mother, aren't they?" Imajin asked.

"Yes," Oriyah whispered tearfully.

"The only reason you're still here is that you're waiting to see if I'm going with you or not?" Imajin asked.

"Yes, but are you reading my energy or my mind?" Oriyah replied jokingly. She added, "Please, I want you to be with me. Everything is ready. My ship and equipment…everything."

"What are you planning to do?" Imajin asked with concern. She then added, "I can feel the rage, Oriyah. Are you sure there are not any other worlds out there where you might want to explore first?

Oriyah replied, "Yes, there is this one unnamed world that I saw in the archives that's completely covered by water. I would love to go exploring there, and maybe I'll get to see what lies beneath the surface."

"Swimming? You want to go swimming?" Imajin asked.

"Yup," Oriyah replied.

Imajin then added, "So you want to swim on a world covered by water without knowing anything about what lies below the surface?"

Oriyah giggled. "Yup."

Imajin shook her head and smiled. "You are a female without fear, aren't you?"

"For the moment," Oriyah answered. "I know what I can do, so there's nothing for me to fear."

Imajin then said, "You also want to go to a planet dominated by men without knowing the full extent of their capabilities."

"Yes," Oriyah answered. "It's what we do."

Skeptical of her intentions, Imajin asked, "I know why, but why now?"

"Because I can't stop thinking about it, even as I lie here talking to you now. I can't forget. You know, it's really weird when you do that."

"Do what?" Imajin asked.

"Refer to things I haven't told you yet," Oriyah replied.

"I'm sorry. It's almost instinctive. Our connection is strong. You can see into my mind as well. However, I haven't failed to notice you didn't answer my question. What is it you plan to do?" said Imajin.

Oriyah retreated her head back into Imajin's chest and said, "I honestly don't know. I would like to know, for sure, if he's still alive."

"And if he's not?" Imajin asked.

"Then…I don't know," Oriyah replied. "Depends on the state of the planet and its female inhabitants."

"So you're not planning on killing this first male you see?" Imajin asked with concern. "We don't know anything about the planet itself. Or its solar system. We know nothing. Has anyone ever surveyed it?"

"Not that I know of. My mother told my teachers to keep Earth out of our data archives," Oriyah replied.

"How long will it take us to get there?" Imajin asked.

"Well, if we open a gateway through the void, we can get there virtually instantly, but if we take the long way at top speed, it'll take two weeks."

"I think we should take the long way," Imajin suggested.

"Me too. I want time to train a bit more," said Oriyah.

Imajin replied, "And I can study and search for what little information we have on the planet."

"I can teach you some combat techniques if you'd like," Oriyah stated.

"I'm not a fighter. I just like to read," Imajin replied. "I will be your guide and see what you're not seeing."

"I like the sound of that," Oriyah replied. "So is that a yes?"

Imajin stared at the ceiling, pretending to take a few moments to think, though she already knew her answer.

"Umm," said Imajin. She then paused briefly, then continued with a grin, "Ummmm."

Oriyah laughed. "Seriously?!"

Imajin smiled playfully. "Where you go, I go… if that is your desire."

Oriyah's sad eyes now matched her smile. She asked anxiously, "Is there anything you need to get before we go? Anything of sentimental value?

"I'm already holding it," Imajin replied before giving Oriyah a kiss on the cheek. "So when do we…"

Before she got a chance to finish, Oriyah put on her cloak, picked her up like an infant, and jumped out the window again, smiling while Imajin screamed from pure shock on the way down. This time the impact barely made an imprint on the ground, as if she were landing on air.

Imajin yelled, "Wait, wait, wait—put me down!"

"What's wrong?" Oriyah asked.

"What do you mean, what's wrong?!" Imajin exclaimed. While grabbing her chest and trying to catch her breath, she added, "You don't just grab someone and jump out a window! At least give me a warning."

Oriyah snickered and said, "I'm sorry."

"You're sorry??!?" Imajin laughed while still trying to catch her breath.

"That's for laughing at me when I fell," Oriyah teased.

Imajin replied, "Oh! That was payback?"

She then looked around at Yoruba's gardens and added, "It's good you didn't make another mess. I would've had to clean it again."

"So you did that?" Oriyah asked. "Thank you."

"You're welcome. Yoruba wanted you to do it!" Imajin replied.

Oriyah laughed and said, "I knew she would." Shen then added, "Are you ready?"

"No, I changed my mind. I'm not going!" Imajin jokingly exclaimed with crossed arms and a side-eye.

"Yes, you are," Oriyah replied.

"I know, but we're walking," Imajin said sternly.

"Aww, really?!? But it's more fun to run," Ori-yah replied.

Imajin replied, "Okay, but I'm getting on your back. You're not carrying me."

Oriyah bent down. "Up you go."

As Imajin went to climb on her back, she said to her MUG, "Ulloa, run diagnostics and prepare the ship for takeoff."

"Wait, who's Ulloa?" Imajin asked.

"The ship's AI," Oriyah replied.

She then took off like a bullet out of a gun. Trees, buildings, and other patrons alike were nothing but a blur. Before Imajin realized it, they were already in their spaceship—so fast it was as if they were teleported there.

Oriyah then said, "Ulloa, let's go."

As the ship launched into orbit, Ulloa asked, "Should I plot a course?"

"Yes. Plot a course for Earth," Oriyah replied.

Ulloa replied, "I'm sorry, but I don't have that planet in my database."

"Ulloa!" Oriyah exclaimed. "Listen, I know who you really are! I know my mother asked you to transfer your consciousness into my ship.

I know your name was once Initri. I understand my mother wants to protect me, but my choices are my own. No one can control my actions other than me. So you either do as I ask, or kindly transfer your consciousness back to my mother. Which will it be?"

"I apologize for the deceit. I will chart a course now," Ulloa replied.

"Thank you," Oriyah responded.

Confused, Imajin asked, "Soooo…we're good to go?"

"Yeah," Oriyah replied as they walked toward the bridge of the ship.

Once there, Imajin looked around and said, "Impressive."

"My own specifications and design. My mother's partner Melvenia built it. A thing of beauty and the first ship of its kind," Oriyah added.

Suddenly Ulloa said, "Opening a portal to Earth."

"No, we shall take the long way," Oriyah responded. "Chart a safe course through the void instead."

They both sat down in the pilot and copilot chairs and stared into the void and marveled at the stars afar as the ship took off and started to accelerate to near the speed of light.

Oriyah asked Ulloa, "So why did my mother send you? Does she not trust me to make sound decisions?"

Ulloa replied, "It's not that at all. She doesn't want you to become her. You are your mother's daughter as she is her mother's daughter.

"What do you mean by 'to become her'? Explain, please," Oriyah responded.

"Your mother knew you wouldn't attend the gathering after she told you the story of her past. She knew you would be angry and seek revenge because it's what she would do...it's what she did," Ulloa replied. She then added, "Her mother and her aunts were critically injured by a powerful, seemingly immortal male entity called Abaddon who attacked them after they had exhausted all their energy when they sank Atlantis into the depths of the oceans to keep the technology out of the hands of man. They fell to injuries after they lived long enough to see that their daughters had learned all they needed to learn to defend themselves in a new world."

"Continue," Oriyah responded.

Ulloa continued, "Thousands of years later, your mother and her sisters hunted him relentlessly and all that followed him. They laid waste to thousands of men and left their heads on pikes, with their decapitated bodies lying below. When they finally found him, they had to fight through a legion of demons and men. The battle lasted for six moons, and on the seventh they finally captured him."

"Did they kill him?" Imajin asked.

"Yes," Ulloa replied, "but first they mercilessly punished him for crippling their mothers. After they'd had their revenge, they dismembered and disemboweled him and burned each part separately until it was nothing but ash. However, they couldn't stop there. You can't just kill the man. You have to kill his ideas…the infection that rots the mind and plagues it with chaos. So they sought out every civilization that praised him by participating in human sacrifice and simply obliterated the entire city. In future years, his name was feared to be said aloud. For the fate of anyone who mentioned it was to be destroyed without pity, women and men alike. His name faded into myth, then became nothing at all. As a group, your mother and her sisters earned the name 'the Manitou.'"

"Wow," Imajin said.

Oriyah added, "How do you know these things?"

Ulloa replied, "Your mother uploaded her memory into my data banks years ago. We were together throughout her journey, and that was her way of trying to get me to evolve to understand emotions more. To see everything she's seen and felt."

Oriyah then stated, "So control…that's what she wants me to learn."

"Initially, yes," Ulloa replied.

"Initially?" Oriyah responded tentatively.

All of a sudden, a voice recording of her mother's voice played back: "Don't let my past pain become your anger." After hearing that, Oriyah stood up and walked away.

"Where are you going?" Imajin asked.

"To train," Oriyah replied.

CHAPTER 8
THE WORLD OF MAN UNTIL NOW…

"A man's world"

W hen they were not snuggling with each other, Oriyah was in the training center pummeling holographic 3D simulations of men, physically and mentally preparing for the whatever lay ahead, while Imajin learned all she could about the inner workings of the ship and the ship's artificial intelligence, Ulloa. She also dug through the archives and found what little information she could find on the planet Earth. As she scrolled through the archives, Imajin said, "Ulloa, you know what happened to Oriyah's mother, right?"

"Yes," Ulloa replied.

Imajin then said, "Tell me everything, please. I need to know in complete detail."

After Imajin heard every detail of Mayri's capture, torture, and murder, the disturbing story let her understand more about how Oriyah was feeling. She knew it was imperative to find out more about Earth. So she asked Ulloa, "Is it possible to open a portal through the void so we could send drones ahead of us to research the planet?"

"Yes," Ulloa answered. "But we're still far away, and there will be an hour delay in transmission due to distance."

"Well, at least we will have gathered some information on the planet's current populace so we're not going in blind...Do it," Imajin responded. "But make sure they are cloaked and undetectable."

Over the next two days, with the help of Ulloa, Imajin went to work on a new and improved bio-suit for her and Oriyah. It was a suit that allowed the imagination to reign supreme, complete with a white cloak laced with golden trim. The suit itself was infused with nanites, which were self-replicating microscopic robots that connected with the wearer's nervous system, enhancing the body as a whole. They could harness and focus their energy to be used as projectiles, instantly construct weapons, and make the user virtually invisible to the naked eye, all the while adapting to any environment. She thought such a thing would be needed for the mission ahead.

As they approached Earth, at first sight they both were in awe of the sheer enchantment and similarity to their planet. The closer they got, the more enchanting it became. Imajin looked at Oriyah and saw not anger or the need for revenge but joy. It was heartwarming to see.

Moments later, while she was gazing at the planet, Imajin's ears started to ring. She flinched when a sharp pain tore through her brain like a painful migraine, followed by an unnerving aura that overwhelmed her body. She looked over at Oriyah to see if she noticed or felt the same, but Oriyah was still gazing at the planet. Imajin didn't know exactly what had happened, but keeping things stable for Oriyah was more important. So she chose to ignore it.

One thing she did notice was Oriyah staring intently at the oceans.

Imajin scoffed and smiled. "Don't you say! Don't you say it!"

"Say what?" Oriyah gushed.

"I can see you staring at the water," Imajin stated.

Oriyah paused and looked at Imajin with the side-eye while trying to hold back a smile. She then mumbled, "Just a quick dip."

Imajin added, "What? I couldn't hear you."

Oriyah added, "Nothing."

"Okay," Imajin replied. "Well, we need to gather information before we do anything."

"I want to swim," Oriyah blurted.

Imajin cried out laughing. "Really? Right now? We literally just got here, and that is the first thing you want to do?"

Oriyah chuckled. "It's so blue. I just want to explore. It wants me to go swimming."

"The water wants you to go swimming?" Imajin asked sarcastically.

"Yes, you don't hear it asking? It's not really asking—it's more like a demand!" Oriyah joked.

Imajin giggled and added, "Well, I guess we have no choice."

"Ulloa, stay here in orbit. We will take one of the detachable pods. Research and observe the area," Oriyah said quickly.

"We?" Imajin exclaimed.

Oriyah looked at her and said, "You really want me to go by myself?"

"No," Imajin replied as she cautiously stared at Earth. When she turned back to look at Oriyah, she had disappeared.

Over the intercom, she heard, "Are you coming?" Oriyah was already in the pod, ready to take off.

When Imajin got to the pod, the door closed behind her. "So where are we headed?"

"Somewhere where there's no land close by," Oriyah replied.

Caution thrown to the wind, Oriyah launched and descended quickly over the Pacific Ocean. As worried as Imajin was, she dared not complicate her moment of joy. When they finally touched down, their pod hovered over the water. Oriyah quickly opened the hatch and took off her cloak. She blew Imajin a kiss and leaped into the water. All Imajin could do was smile as she watched Oriyah leap in and out of the water like a dolphin.

Meanwhile, waiting for Oriyah to finish her business exploring and frolicking with sea creatures, Imajin checked her MUG to see how much information had been gathered. She accessed one of the drones and started to analyze the data collected. When she scrolled through Earth's history, to her shock, one of the first images and descriptions was something that Oriyah wouldn't take too well. Before she could come to terms with this newfound information, loud thumping noises started to resonate all around her. The sounds got louder and louder, indicating the fact that whatever it is was getting closer.

Moments later, two helicopters carrying heavily armed soldiers geared for war started converging on her location. They hovered around her, yelling over the loudspeaker, "Do not move—you are trespassing on American soil. Surrender or you will be fired upon." Not knowing much about the planet, Imajin didn't quite understand their demands. Frightened, she went to touch the button that would close the hatch, but before she could, Oriyah rose out of the water like she had wings and landed on the top of the pod.

Worried about Imajin, she asked, "Are you okay?"

"Yes...they just scared me," Imajin replied.

"Well, I'm here now. I'm sorry I was gone for so long," said Oriyah.

She then looked around at the helicopters and the soldiers pointing their weapons at them with a maleficent grin on her face and her hands clasped behind her back. She was completely and eerily calm, showing no fear at all. This is the moment she had wanted from the beginning but did not want to entice because the rage might grow to be uncontrollable.

She thought to herself, You started it.

The soldiers repeated, "Do not move, or you will be fired upon."

She kept smiling and told Imajin, "Close the hatch."

Imajin didn't say a word; she just closed the hatch. Immediately, gunfire from an Apache attack helicopter rained down upon them. After seemingly hitting nothing but air, the soldiers were terror-struck. Not understanding what was happening, they all panicked and started to launch missiles and gunfire simultaneously.

After a barrage of bullets and missiles, the smoke and fire steadily cleared. When they did, the highly aggressive soldiers noticed an energy force field covering not only her but the pod as well. In haste they continued firing until they had no more ammunition. When all was said and done, Oriyah remained calm as a summer evening before night begins.

She laughed, mocking their futile attempt to destroy someone they didn't even know. Afterward, her body started to glow. A gathering of light started in her chest before engulfing her entire body. Following that, the energy made its way to her left hand. She raised her palm, and the energy transformed into a ball that started to rotate.

The fear in their eyes was satisfying, and with a smile she whispered to herself, "So power is what you fear. When you don't have it." She then started playfully tossing the ball up and down in the air, and on the fourth toss, it didn't come down. The ball of energy halted midair. Then without warning it split into multiple pieces and disintegrated the helicopters, leaving the soldiers inside uninjured.

As they floated helplessly, Oriyah stepped down off the roof of the pod and stood on the surface of the water. Seeing that, the soldiers immediately started frantically swimming away.

She laughed out loud and said, "Where are you going? There is no land near here." She walked to one of the soldiers and grabbed him by the head and picked him up out of the water and asked, "Who sent you?"

Without hesitation the soldiers said, "We're with the US Navy. We were told that an unidentified object touched down here, and we were ordered to investigate."

She then asked, "Who ordered you?"

"We don't really know. We just follow the orders of higher-ranked officers," the soldier answered. He then pleaded, "Please, we were just following orders." Without warning, a bullet from a soldier's pistol struck her in the side. She flinched, dropping the man back into the water. Holding her side, she said "So that's what they feel like" while peeling the bullet out of her biosuit.

She chuckled while looking at the soldier that did it. "You tried to steal my life." She walked over to the man as he emptied the clip, hitting nothing but a force field. She grasped the top of his head and picked him up out of the water. She looked into his eyes and smiled while releasing her grip. Before his body hit the water, she cut off his head with an energy-based sword that cauterized the wound upon contact, leaving no blood. His body hit the water and sank, while his head floated around with a surprised look on its dead face.

Oriyah nudged the floating head with her foot while glaring at the others before walking back to the pod. For a moment the soldiers felt relief, thinking they were in the clear, until their bodies stiffened and suddenly rose slowly out of the water as if they were being pulled into the air.

With her arm extended, Oriyah seemed to lift the men without touching them. She then slowly started to make a fist. Meanwhile, the soldiers' bones started cracking and breaking. As they cried out from the pain, both Oriyah and Imajin noticed that one of their cries was not the cry of a man. When Oriyah realized one of the soldiers was female, she stopped, dropping everyone except the woman back in the water.

While Oriyah glared at the woman menacingly, Imajin quickly opened the hatch and said "We're taking her with us," knowing there was a good possibility that Oriyah was thinking about killing her.

Without arguing, she lowered the woman gently inside their pod. Afterward, she turned her attention back to the soldiers. Now anger had taken over because a woman was helping male kind destroy another woman. She made their deaths painful. Not only to satisfy herself but also to give the female soldier something else to remember.

Again she raised her hand, and the soldiers rose out of the water. Their bodies stiffened, and their bones broke as they seized up from the pain while choking on their own blood.

As Oriyah was about to get back into the pod, they could hear more helicopters approaching. She looked around and started smiling again.

"Nope," Imajin shouted. "Let's go, now!"

Oriyah growled while pouting like a baby and said, "Okay." She closed the hatch and took off.

Upon their return to their ship, Imajin was completely astonished at Oriyah's abilities. "Well, I guess we lost the element of surprise," Imajin added

"Oh, I think they were surprised," Oriyah jokingly added. They both shared a laugh as the female soldier in the back remained momentarily too terrified to move. Oriyah looked at her and sarcastically said, "Those were your people, right?"

"Oriyah," Imajin said sternly.

"What? I was just asking," Oriyah added.

"I know what you're doing. Stop it," Imajin exclaimed.

"Okay," Oriyah replied.

Imajin turned to the woman and said, "We're not going to hurt you. We just need your help." After playfully slapping Oriyah on the leg, she added, "We don't harm females."

Still terrified, not only by the fact that she'd been abducted by aliens and her fellow soldiers had been killed in front of her but also by the fact that she was now in space, headed to their mother ship, she uttered, "Okay."

Oriyah added, "Even though you tried to harm me."

Imajin glared at her.

Upon seeing the look on her face, Oriyah said, "Okay, I'm done."

"Anyway, how was your swim?" Imajin asked.

"Disgusting," Oriyah answered. "The water is slightly toxic, and I don't know why, but I intend on finding out."

"That's why she's here," Imajin said. "We need to know about the females and the state of the world. We can read about it, but we need someone who has experienced life here." She turned to the woman. "What is your name?"

"Natalie," the woman replied. She then added, "And who are you? Where are you from?"

Imajin answered as their pod docked with the main ship. "My name is Imajin, and this is Oriyah, and we're from a world far away from this one. Come with us, please."

Now inside their ship, Natalie was amazed at the fascinating advanced technology on display. Millions of questions ran through her mind, but she asked only one. "Why are you here?"

"To destroy the planet," Oriyah joked.

"Stop!" Imajin exclaimed with a playful slap on her arm. "Look at her—she's already terrified, and you want to frighten her even more?" she added. "We're here to observe the state of your world. And help the women who want it. You have nothing to fear from us. I just want to ask you some questions, and we will let you go. You're not a prisoner. You're a guest. You can sit down."

"So you're just going to let me go? Just like that…?" Natalie replied.

"Yes. As I said before, we don't hurt females— but male kind, now that's different," Imajin replied, alleviating her worries. She added, "Are you injured?"

"No, I don't think so, but I think I'm in a state of shock. So it's hard to tell," Natalie answered.

"Well, let's just be sure," Imajin replied. Natalie flinched, frightened, as Imajin tried to place her hand on top of her head.

Imajin responded with a soothing tone to her voice, "Be still. Be calm...I won't hurt you."

Natalie gasped in shock as Imajin's hand started to glow. She, along with Oriyah, was astonished with what was currently happening.

"Your left and right arm, in addition to your ribs, had small fractures, but they're good now," Imajin added.

"How did you do that?" Natalie and Oriyah asked simultaneously.

"I don't know," Imajin replied. She glanced at Oriyah and added, "I told you—it's all becoming instinctive. My body just reacts. I can't explain it."

Oriyah smiled proudly. She knew what was happening even if Imajin didn't. The more she trusted intuition and instinct, the closer they brought her to the realization of who she truly was, a daughter of the celestial mother. A powerful being of light that would exceed her belief in her own capabilities. Oriyah could not wait to see what was next for her partner.

Suddenly Natalie jumped up and excitedly asked, "What else did you do? Because I feel... good. Better than good. I feel great. Thank you."

Imajin replied, "It was my privilege. We didn't know a female was among those males."

"That's because her frequency is different from that of other females. They've been corrupted," Oriyah snipped as she walked to the training room. "Come to me after you finish questioning this"—she scoffed and finished condescendingly—"female."

After Oriyah left, Natalie said, "It seems as though she really doesn't like me."

"Well, you did try and steal her life," Imajin replied.

"I was just following orders," Natalie added.

"Funny, that man said the same thing," Imajin countered. "I wonder—why do you follow them?"

"It's my job. I do as I'm ordered," Natalie replied.

"And that makes you happy?" Imajin asked.

"It makes me happy to serve my county and set up a financially stable future for myself in the process," Natalie replied.

"Country, financially...I'm not yet familiar with those words. What does that mean?" Imajin asked.

Natalie explained, "Well, I'm a soldier in my country's air force, America. We have different branches of the military that respond to different threats to our national security. We all protect our country from foreign invaders. It's an honor to serve."

She then asked, "You don't have to pay for things where you're from? Things like water, lights, food, and medicine?" Natalie asked.

"Why would you have to pay for something that is free? Our entire society is beneficial to all its inhabitants," Imajin answered.

"Wow! I would love to meet the man behind that," Natalie replied.

"Man!" Imajin exclaimed. "No, why would we bring chaos to the natural world? That's just...stupid. No, it's just us females. Females of different origins and species living together happily."

"What?! And do they all have powers like you and her?" Natalie wondered.

Imajin smiled and said, "Yes, depending on the individual—it's natural for us. As it should be for you."

"No woman on Earth can do the things I've seen the two of you do," said Natalie.

"I wonder why that is," Imajin replied. She then added, "As Oriyah said before, your frequency is different from that of the females on our world."

"Frequency? Like radio frequencies?" Natalie asked.

Imajin giggled and said, "No, your bio frequency. Females are all connected to an ancient stream of energy that connects us all in one way or another. So we can sense or sometimes hear the thoughts of other females close by."

"That sounds annoying. Women bicker too much. Too much judgment. I myself have more male friends than female," Natalie responded.

"Hmm…that's odd, but it does explain a lot," said Imajin. "So you're comfortable here with men?"

"Not completely, no…a small percentage of them are kind, but most are not. Well, it's a gamble sometimes. What you thought was a good, honest man could turn out to be the complete opposite," Natalie answered. "It's unsafe to be a woman of any age in today's world."

"And knowing that, you still choose to have more male friends," Imajin stated. "You don't think of all your male friends. That one day one of them or more than one of them could just snap and try and take something from you that never belonged to them."

Natalie paused briefly and pondered before saying, "I don't know...maybe."

"So you gamble your life on a maybe...hmm. Might want to be careful with that," Imajin added.

"We don't really have much of a choice here. The world is ruled by man. We have to adapt. In some countries women can't even go outside without a man with them," Natalie stated. She then added, "Every culture revolves around men. It's their world. We just live in it."

"Explain," Imajin added.

"I wouldn't know where to start. It'll take all day to do that," Natalie replied.

"Tell me something I should know as a female entering your society. We have time," said Imajin.

Natalie thought for a moment before she passionately said, "Women are raped or tortured every second of every day. Even while we sit here talking, women are abducted and sold into sex slavery, which, by the way, is the most profitable criminal enterprise in the entire world. We also have to live in fear that the men we choose might just up and kill us one day if we get into an argument or have a slight disagreement."

"Sex slavery—what is that? Tell me more," Imajin interrupted.

Gazing at the seriousness in her eyes, Natalie replied without hesitation, "It's a criminal enterprise of men who literally kidnap millions of women and little girls all over the world to sell them to others all over the world to do as they please. Most are killed after their usefulness runs out."

"And nobody's doing anything about this?" Imajin angrily asked, as it reminded her of her own planet.

Natalie replied, "It involves men with money and power to do whatever they want. Some people try, but they don't get very far."

"Ulloa!" Imajin shouted.

"Yes," Ulloa replied.

"Did you hear her?" Imajin asked.

"Yes," Ulloa answered.

"Find any information you can! And notify me when you do!" Imajin demanded. Calming herself, she turned her focus back to Natalie, and with a patronizing tone, she said, "Tell me more about this world of yours where you have more male friends than female friends and are content with living in an unsafe world where little girls are being abducted and raped every day."

All of a sudden, Ulloa announced, "Drone data collection complete. Search for abducted women still underway."

Imajin said, "Let me see for myself. You can just sit here and think about the world you're living in."

Natalie asked, "What are you about to do?"

"Go over the details of your planet," Imajin answered as she sat down at the communications console.

"Careful," Ulloa cautioned. "Their history is deceitful and chaotic. It could damage your spirit."

Without heeding her warning, Imajin put a device on her head that let her mentally download

the collected information. Natalie watched silently as she slipped into a hypnotic state. She also
observed some of the images and words that rapidly passed by on a three-dimensional holographic interface. She saw flashes of the history of her
own world, including some of the bombs she was
ordered to drop for the contradictory notion of
freedom. However, she felt no remorse because
it was her job, and her job was to do whatever the
commanding officer commanded.

Imajin was being fed the complete horrifying
and saddening data of Earth. Without blinking,
every few seconds her entire body would slightly
twitch, signifying the emotions she felt while re-
ceiving a history of war and pain while the female
was nothing more than a second thought, if that!
Seconds later, water filled her eyes as she finally
blinked, and a single tear slid down her face. A
few minutes of dead silence passed by while Imajin remained in a trance, undergoing the down-
loading of information on Earth's history.

Suddenly, a loud beeping noise interrupted the
process. "What is it?" Imajin exclaimed with frustration. Without answering, Ulloa pulled up a live
video feed from just one of the drones still roam-

ing Earth and it seemed they had gotten there just in time.

They saw a beautiful mansion with three well-dressed men hanging out on an equally beautiful back porch, having drinks and chatting without a care in the world as more than a few armed guards patrolled the outer grounds. It would seem nothing was out of the ordinary, except the conversation took a turn for the worse...for a woman.

"So where's the ladies?" one of the men asked their host.

"Yeah, you already fucked us on this deal. So now let some girls finish the job!" The other guy added.

The host laughed and said confidently, "Sean, Jeff, my friends, oh boy do I have a treat for you!"

"Better be a good damn treat!" Sean replied jokingly.

"I remember what you like," the host replied.

Moments later, he clapped his hands, and one of the guards came running. "Yes, boss," the guard responded.

"Bring them up," he replied. "Are they fresh?"

"Uh, yeah," the guard replied.

"What the hell does that mean?" Sean said with a bit of concern. "I can't bring anything back to my wife."

"Me either," Jeff agreed.

"Explain," the host demanded angrily.

"It was short notice, boss. We did the best we could," the guard replied.

The host stood up and assertively approached him and said, "And what is your best?"

"They're clean, boss. I promise you. We've had them for a few weeks," he answered.

"Weeks! These girls go through dozens of men a day, and you want me to fuck one of them?" the host replied. "I told you I wanted them to be fresh!"

"Katya has been out all day. She couldn't get anyone to come with her," the guard replied. "All we could get was a set of twin girls."

The host shook his head and said, "I don't care if they're twins. I wanted them fresh, untouched!"

"They haven't been touched, boss," the guard replied, reassuring his employer. "They're probably ten years old. Fresh stock. We can make a lot of money off them."

"I call dibs," Jeff blurted.

"Noooooo, they're mine," Sean added with a distasteful smile.

"Bring them out, but put the twins in Sean's room," the host replied.

"Ah, come on!" Jeff said disappointedly.

Sean laughed and said, "Too bad for you."

A few minutes later, the guard aggressively led the trafficked women onto the porch and forcibly lined them up, as if they were in a beauty pageant.

"Not bad," Sean exclaimed with slight excitement.

"A little of everything," Jeff added.

At the same time, the host nodded his head in approval and said to himself, "Not bad at all."

"Smell test," Jeff added. "Ten fingers, more than enough for all of you."

Seconds later, he stood up and walked around the women, inspecting the merchandise. Afterward he proceeded to aggressively grope each of them while stuffing his hands down their pants and smelling his fingers.

"Not bad," he repeated. "I'd fuck them all."

They laughed like they were having the time of their lives, but the look on each woman's face was the complete opposite. The men laughed at their tears and were aroused by the fact that they were frightened, without any choice in what was about to happen to their bodies. Male kind loved to control anything and everything they could.

Now, in their own rooms with the women, they chose to make them meet their every demand.

Sean, the one who was gifted the two little girls, was preparing himself for a despicable act.

He started by making the twins get on their knees and crawl to him.

"Like a baby," he said with a disturbing grin.

Their terrified shaking was accompanied by a continual stream of tears. The twins held each other's hands and stood in place. He slapped one of them and said, "If you don't do what I say, I will kill her, and if you don't do what I say, I'll kill her," knowing that their love for each other would force them to do as he asked without resistance.

Sean walked to the bed, turned around, and added, "Now crawl to me. Like a baby," he repeated.

The girls reluctantly got on their knees and started to crawl, and suddenly a lot of commotion started outside his door.

Moments later, the host barged into Sean's room, scared out of his mind, as two guards protected the entrance and the other protected their boss.

"What's going on?!" Sean exclaimed.

"I don't know," he replied. "Jeff's dead! The cars are gone, and most of the guards are dead!"

"How?! What happened?!" Sean shouted.

"I don't know," the host yelled back.

There were a few seconds of worried, panicky silence.

"Blood," the guard said. "So much blood, and body parts everywhere."

"What the hell is he talking about?" Sean yelled.

Suddenly the guard's radio started crackling as painful cries nearly burst the radio itself. Following that, they heard the sound of a man gurgling on his own blood before a violent, swift slashing sound brought more than a lot of concern to each of them.

"What the fuck?!" Sean blurted. "It sounds like he's being ripped apart."

Without notice, every light in the mansion simultaneously shut off. Only a speck of light from a distant streetlight illuminated the bedroom.

"Stay here," the guard ordered before joining the others protecting the entrance.

Meanwhile, outside the door, the men stood firmly ready to protect their boss, but no amount of ammunition could've prepared them for this moment.

As they glared down the long, dark, empty hallway waiting for whatever was brutally killing the other guards, the head guard asked, "Did any of you see anything?"

"No, I just heard the screams," another guard replied.

All of a sudden, a faint clicking noise reverberated throughout the mansion.

"You hear that?" the guard asked, panicked and slightly hysterical. He added, "I'm getting the fuck out of here!"

As he ran down the dark hallway, midstride, his head suddenly detached from his body, and then there was a quick slash through his waist.

The remaining two looked on in terror as the head rolled toward their feet.

Peering into the eyes and seeing the last petrified look on his face, they instantly started firing down the hallway, hitting everything in sight until their clips were empty, but the faint clicking sound continued.

The men were scared stiff, as if their legs were glued to the floor. The guns they were holding rattled from fear of the unknown.

Unexpectedly the clicking noise got louder, signifying that whatever it is, was getting much closer.

"What do we do?" one of the last guards asked.

"Hold your position!" the other exclaimed.

Before long, a light trickling sound of fear-stricken urine pummeled the marble floor.

"Are you serious?" the head guard said disappointedly.

"I'm sor—" His reply was cut off midsentence as blood spilled to the floor from an unseen foe that split open his stomach, releasing everything inside.

The blood splattered all over the last remaining guard. As he whipped the debris from his face and eyes, a brutal strike lacerated his face before another devastating blow pierced his sternum, sending him flying backward and violently forcing the door wide open.

His lifeless body hit the floor and slid toward the last two remaining well-dressed men.

As Jeff vomited from disgust, their host picked up the dead guard's sidearm in a futile attempt to protect himself. After which, he grabbed one of the twins, yanking her away from her sister to use the child as a human shield.

"Whoever you are, I can pay you!" the host frantically yelled. "I can give you whatever you want. I can make you rich. Just let us go!"

As he was on his knees, trying to clean the vomit from his face, a splatter of blood forced Jeff to look up to see his host's skin start to boil, as if someone had poured acid all over his body.

The little girl broke free and joined her sister as they both huddled in fear in the corner. The host's body continued to melt gradually, revealing the muscle and bone below his skin, until he was a pile of something that resembled Jeff's own vomit.

Jeff quickly stood up and backed away, and at that moment his legs were cut from under him.

He cried out in tremendous pain before the unknown entity slowly revealed itself. Like it was stepping from the shadows while revealing itself to the light.

It was a being covered from head to toe in silver and gold while wearing a white hooded cloak. It divulged its face to be humanoid, with multicolored skin and the features of a woman. Her eyes were that of fire as she said nonchalantly, "Now crawl to me."

"Please, I'm sorry," Jeff pleaded.

She turned to the frightened twins and said, "Please don't fear me. I would never harm you."

Before turning her attention back to the legless man, she then repeated, "If you want to live, crawl to me."

He instantly started weeping, hearing what he himself had demanded of the twins.

In the midst of his crawling and whimpering like a wounded animal, she plunged a blade into his hand, pinning him to the floor.

Following that, the material that covered her body started to vibrate as her fingers transformed into serrated claws. She then very slowly dug her fingers into his back as he cried out in agony.

Legless, with a blade stuck into his hand while her claws settled into his back, he continued to plead, "Please, I'm begging you."

She flipped him over and said, while peering into his frightened, teary eyes, "Your words are nothing but manipulation."

As she clutched the back of his head, she pulled him in close and bored her finger into his eye. Curving her finger as if pulling the trigger of a gun, she ripped out his nasal cavity and tossed it across the room. His last moment of life was as painful as the pain he had intended to force upon the twins.

Seconds later, after watching the man die grue- somely, she approached the girls and knelt in front of them and said calmly, "My name is Imajin. I won't hurt you." She was reassuring the twins of their safety, but as soon as they were set at ease, something came crashing through the ceiling.

When the dust settled, it was Oriyah, standing ready, but the action was already over and done with.

She looked around at the decapitated bodies and said with sarcasm, "So it's okay when you do it but a problem when I think about doing it?"

"You couldn't just get Ulloa to open a passage here?" Imajin shouted. "You really had to crash through the ceiling?"

Oriyah snickered and said, "Did I scare you?"

"Yes...yes you did!" Imajin exclaimed. She added, "Now go downstairs and get the other women and don't frighten them. They've been through enough."

After retrieving the other women, they gathered around outside the mansion. "Where is the other one?" Imajin asked.

"I didn't see anyone else," Oriyah replied.

"There is another. She's locked herself in the bathroom," one of the trafficked women replied.

"Why?" Oriyah questioned.

"Because she is a part of their group, and all of us are here mainly because of her," she replied.

Oriyah angrily growled and vanished. Shortly after, she reappeared as if by magic, holding the woman by her throat. The all gasped in shock as her feet dangled in the air.

"Let her go," Imajin yelled.

"Why? She is just as bad as male kind," Oriyah replied.

"We don't harm females, my love. It's not what we do, remember?" Imajin responded. "Let's get these women to safety."

Oriyah released her throat, and she fell hard to the ground. "Pathetic," Oriyah added while looking down at her.

After a few moments of awkward silence, a portal opened near them as the sirens from law enforcement closed in on their location in response to the gunfire.

"Please come with us," Imajin pleaded, "or you can stay here and do what you want. The choice is yours."

Not only were the trafficked women concerned about the real intention of these warrior women, but a magical portal was also enough to cause the women to be reluctant to do anything they asked. However, the twins' reaction was completely different.

As a window can been seen through both sides, the portal functioned the same way, and the twins didn't hesitate to grab Imajin's hand while waiting to follow her through. Seeing how joyful and easy the children were, the others followed suit.

"And what about her?" said Oriyah, referring to Katya, the one who helped men find young women to exploit.

"What do you mean? She is coming with us!" Imajin exclaimed as she and the others walked into the portal.

After they were all safely through the portal, Oriyah took it upon herself to scrawl the words "NO MORE SHALL SHE ENDURE" on the walls using one of the severed arms of the fallen.

CHAPTER 9
HER STORY

"Survivor stories"

On the other side of the portal, the kids were weirdly calm, but the others suddenly became hysterical once they realized they were on a spaceship. "Where are we? What did you do to us?" they asked.

"You're somewhere they will never find you or harm you ever again!" Imajin replied.

"Why did you bring her here?" another asked, referring to Katya.

Oriyah answered, "Because she could reveal more locations of women in the same predicament. Don't you want those women to be rescued?"

"Yes," the woman replied.

Oriyah added, "It is my mission to rescue women from the chaos of males. So trust me—as long as you're here, no man will ever harm you."

After moments of trying to calm themselves, one of the women slowly made her way to the window. "Are we really in space?"

"We simply refer to it as the void, but…yes. We are in controlled orbit," Oriyah answered.

Imajin then added, "So will you trust us? Please know we would never do anything to hurt you or tell you anything false. Please."

In unison, the twins blurted joyfully, "We trust you."

Finally hearing their soft little voices, Imajin smiled, knelt in front of them, and said, "Thank you for your trust. I will never betray it."

Noticing how gracious Imajin was to such a simple answer, the women responded, "Yes."

Imajin turned to them and said, "Thank you."

"Ulloa, can you scan them, please?" Oriyah asked.

"I already have," Ulloa replied.

"And?" Oriyah replied.

Ulloa continued, "They all have multiple sexually transmitted diseases. Two of them are HIV positive. They have multiple improperly healed fractures and broken bones, in addition to fractured pelvic bones and multiple contusions, and their blood is heavy with opiates."

The women gasped in shock, but before they had a chance to say anything, Imajin added, "And the healing waters of Niribu can cure all that."

"Healing waters? This may be a dumb question, but will it be painful?" one of the women asked with concern.

"Of course not," Imajin replied, easing her worries. "Please just follow me, and I will show you."

They came upon a room with white walls, with golden words inscribed around a small three-foot-deep pool that was placed directly in the center. "I need you to take off your clothing and submerge yourselves in the water for a while," said Oriyah.

"A while?!?!" a woman blurted. "How will we breathe?"

Another added, "And why do we need to take off our clothes?"

"The waters breathe for you, and because your clothes hold remnants of trauma. Your body needs to be bare," Oriyah replied. "We will give you more garments to wear once the process is over."

Before the women finished asking their questions, the twins playfully cannonballed into pool. Following the kids' example, the women looked to one another and gradually started to unclothe.

"Now tell us your names and how you found yourselves in this situation," Imajin chimed in.

While they were reluctantly taking off their garments, one of the four replied, "I guess I will go first. My name is Farrah."

"And how did you get there, Farrah?" Imajin asked.

"My father sold me when I was nine years old for $300, and I was forced to marry the brutal leader of the Taliban, who beat and raped me daily. He died a few years later when the Americans attacked. I thought all was well until I was raped repeatedly by their soldiers and sold into slavery when they were done with me." She smirked in contempt and added, "I worshipped my father, and $300 is what I was worth to him."

"I know the feeling," another woman said. She then said, "My mother died when I was three, and my father started molesting me soon after, but he didn't start having sex with me until a little later. First, he wanted to teach me to please him by forcing me to watch pornography and give him oral while he watched little girls' beauty pageants." She added, "I tried to run away, but he caught me and locked me in the basement. He beat me mercilessly, and he raped me, but when I got older, he wouldn't touch me. He only liked younger girls, but that didn't stop him from selling me to his friends." She then added, "My name is Elizabeth, by the way."

"But how did you end up here?" Oriyah asked.

"I honestly can't remember. I went to sleep and woke up in a different cage," Elizabeth replied.

Next, another woman joined in. "My name is Ying. I grew up in a very small village. I always read western fables of the white knight that saves the damsel in distress, and I wanted to be her." She continued, "I was gullible enough to believe in the words of a man I thought was that knight. We met on social media. We talked for almost a year before we actually met. He seemed like a sweet, honest man…a British man. He helped get me to America, and I thought my life was going to be just like the fairy tales. When we met face to face, it was what I thought was love at first sight. But when he got me back to his penthouse apartment, a group of men was waiting for him… or me. I didn't know what was happening." She continued, "I was a virgin, and they gang-raped me while videotaping the whole thing. It went on for a few weeks until one day someone took me from him as a payment for money he owed, and that's how I wound up here."

"We both fell for someone we shouldn't have," the last woman added. "I fell for a sweet, beautiful, and what I thought was an honest person. But she turned out to be worse than the men I feared. My mother brought me across the border from Guatemala when I was five. She was murdered by her boyfriend when I was ten, and I was sold by the police to a couple that brutalized me for years.

"Then when I was twelve, I ran away and was brutally gang-raped and left for dead. I spent months in the hospital recovering and the remainder of my teen years in a mental institute. After I was released, I got an apartment and became a recluse. I didn't go anywhere. Anything I had to do I did online.

"Until one day, I wanted to overcome my fear of the outside world, and I went to a sports bar. It was daytime, so I wasn't as scared as long as I knew I could make it back home before nightfall." She smiled. "But when I got there, I met this amazing woman, and we shared a cerveza. She was so kind and sweet, and we connected in a way that I'd never connected with anyone before.

I was so drawn to her I didn't realize the sun had gone down.

"But I wasn't scared—I was hopeful and at peace because I'd met her." Tears rolled down her face as she glared at Katya. "The last thing I remember saying to her was 'You are the best thing that has happened in my life.'

"And then I woke up…in a room, tied to a bed, as they filled me up with heroin…while she cowered in the corner as if she didn't care at all." She added, "False love."

Katya cried out, "I'm so sorry, Lucia, but they…"

"Don't ever say my name again!" Lucia exclaimed, interrupting her midsentence. "I don't care for your reason. Not even a little bit. They wanted to know how I wound up in that situation, and I told them. That is all."

Oriyah was already angered by their stories, and now she was hearing of a woman using compassion as a way to manipulate someone. That was a trait that male kind had perfected. She glared at Katya with complete disdain.

Moving on, Imajin said, "And you? You look to be only a little older than the twins."

"I'm thirteen," the girl stated. "I was grabbed by some men in ski masks on my way from school. My mother was working late, as usual. She was working two jobs so I could go to a good school, in a good neighborhood, and get a good education. My mama is everything to me, and I'm everything to her. That is why she named me Amoura. It means 'love.'" She then asked, "Will you take me home, please?"

"Yes, of course, Amoura. You are not a prisoner here. I just want to help heal you of your pain. Then you can do as you please," Imajin answered.

Amoura excitedly replied "Thank you" before she embraced Imajin.

Imajin then said to the twins patiently waiting in the pool, gently splashing water on each other, "What about you two? What are your names?"

They stared back at Imajin and smiled while not saying a single word.

"They're Tallulah and Chenoa," Katya replied.

The twins grinned and nodded their heads in agreement.

Imajin then said to all of them, "Now can you all step into the pool?" She added, "Once you do, you're going to feel sleepy, but it's just the water doing what it's supposed to do. The body heals quicker when you're at rest."

Afterward, the women stepped into the pool and started to float on their backs. Within seconds they fell into a deep sleep and sank to the bottom. It was almost as if they had died, but the fact that their chests kept expanding and retracting showed the water was in fact breathing for each of them. Their heartbeats slowed as the pool continually pulsated. Like a current, the water swirled around their bodies, pulling the darkness from their spirits, causing the water itself to become more murky than pristine.

During that time, Oriyah focused her attention on Natalie and Katya and said, "Now you two follow us."

As they did, Natalie asked, "why didn't you heal them like you did me?"

"Because you are a female who fights with male kind. That means you took on their ways. So it's possible you would deceive me," Imajin replied.

"I still don't understand," Natalie added.

"I can sense people's intents, and when I touch them, I can see into their minds and get flashes of their memories."

Natalie paused and stuttered "I...I...I," worried about what Oriyah had seen.

Oriyah raised her hand, gesturing for her to remain silent. She then added, "You don't belong with us. Your spirituality reeks of man."

"What would you have us do? We had to adapt," Katya joined in as they reached the ship's lounge.

Oriyah added, "So that's what you were doing? Adapting to your situation by making Lucia fall for you? Luring women and little girls and putting them through such misery?"

"You don't get it! You don't understand what some of us go through," Katya exclaimed.

"Then by all means...share with me the life that made you betray others like yourself to the world of sex slavery," Oriyah sarcastically stated.

"What for?" Katya asked. She then added, "It seems like you wouldn't care even if I told you."

Imajin joined in: "How can we try and see things from your perspective if we don't know you?"

After a brief moment of silence, with her back against the wall of the ship, she sat down on the ground, knees tucked firmly into her chest, and said, "Living this life is all I know. That's all I can remember. I don't know my mother or my father. I've been in this life so long that my body is of no more use, only my face."

"What does that mean?" Oriyah asked.

"I'm a woman, so it makes it easier for other women to trust me," Katya answered.

"And your body?" Imajin asked.

Katya sobbed and paused for a moment as she explained. "My body is broken, and my insides are unusable. Being drugged every day and being forced to have sex with numerous sadistic men has left me torn up."

"Torn up?" Oriyah asked.

Katya gazed into her eyes and said as tears fell down her face, "For their pleasure, I've been whipped, been cut, had cigarettes put out on my skin, and been penetrated with different sharp objects." With a chill she shakenly added, "I was raped with the broken leg of a chair once, and when I didn't scream enough he raped me with a knife. My entire body…inside and out…hurts every second of every day."

"Knowing what you've been through, why subject other women and children to the same life?" Imajin asked.

Katya sighed sadly and said, "One day, a priest came into the brothel I was living in and chose me to be his pleasure for the evening. I honestly thought my prayers had been answered, but he was the worst of all the men I have ever been with." Katya quietly sobbed with her hands covering her ears while she rocked back and forth, as if the memory itself brought back the pain and panic from that moment. "The things he did to me… please don't make me say them."

"Calm down," Imajin said as she comforted Katya in her arms. "You don't have to."

Katya then added, "After that I made a deal with them. I know what I was doing was wrong, but I just couldn't go back to that man. I couldn't do anything anymore. I tried asking plenty of people for help to get out, but nobody cared…man or woman. Nobody cared, so I stopped caring."

After hearing Katya's and the others' stories, Imajin and even Oriyah were holding back tears, along with an influx of destructive rage. Oriyah felt bad for her comments and recent judgment because she now could understand that Katya's choice was made out of pure desperation. A woman who knew only pain and living life as a slave could force other women to do things that, at first, they thought they would never do.

Now with a certain heartfelt sentiment toward Katya, Oriyah asked her, "Well, now you have someone that does want to help you. Whatever happens now is your choice. What is it you want to do?"

"I don't know," Katya replied. "What is there for me to do?"

Oriyah added, "Save women like you."

"I can't do what you do. I'm not strong," Katya said.

"You've been through a tremendous amount of pain, and you're still here. That's strength," Oriyah added while looking over at Imajin. "She said the same thing, but look at her now."

"I don't know," Katya replied. "My body just can't do it."

"Well, if your body could…what would you do?" said Oriyah.

Katya momentarily contemplated the idea, but before she gave an answer, Oriyah interrupted. "Don't answer yet. Come with us." She then added, "No, you stay here. Ulloa, watch her until we come back," referring to Natalie.

They led Katya back to the healing waters and instructed her to do the same as the others. While she was taking off her clothes, Oriyah and Imajin saw the horrific scarring all over her body. Her back was riddled with long lashes from a whip, and there were long cuts on her breasts. Her genital area looked chewed, with burns on her inner thighs all the way up to her navel.

None of them had ever seen anything like this before. However, it brought back painful memories of Oriyah's mother, the sight that had plagued her mind ever since she'd left home. She then took Katya's hand as Katya stepped into the water and lay down.

As she dozed off, Oriyah tearfully added, "I'm sorry—maybe we can find this priest after you're done. Maybe make him feel a bit...helpless."

Katya cracked a smile as she closed her eyes and sank to the bottom.

Afterward, they returned to the flight deck, and Oriyah said to Natalie, "You tried to steal my life, yes, but maybe I was too quick to judge the lives and hardships of the women who live here. I've met only seven of you, and those seven have had a horrifying experience. It seems you had no choice but to conform." She added, "So I'm going to give you a choice instead of sending you back to the male-dominated life you're used to. What would you like to do…stay or go?"

Natalie asked, "What am I going to do if I stay?"

Oriyah answered, "Whatever you want to do. I would hope that you would help us change the dynamic of your society. What are you going to do if you go?"

"Probably be debriefed about what happened, and they will surely want more information on you. You're a threat now…so they have to eradicate you. Most likely they will try to capture and experiment on the both of you, along with reverse engineering any of your technology to use for their own interest. I'd probably be imprisoned and tested for any pathogens. They wouldn't let me go."

Oriyah replied, "Knowing this, you still choose to fight for or with them?"

Natalie smirked, shook her head. "Like Katya said…you don't quite get it."

"I get that they were forced. You seemed to do it willingly," Oriyah replied.

Imajin chimed in, "My love, I have been through most of their history, and it's full of chaos."

"Then please explain it to me," Oriyah replied.

Imajin then explained, "This world has a hierarchy, and for thousands of years man has been at the top. This world may be full of beauty, but beneath the glamor…it's repulsive."

Natalie added, "I'm going to give you some facts that I've learned through my ten years of service: men hold all the political, social, and economic power, and they get to enforce whatever rhetoric they deem necessary. A bunch of soft women can't win against the brutality of men. We're at odds with society as a whole. We can't win…it's impossible to change something when you have no power. She added sternly, "WE CAN'T WIN."

"Yes, we can," Oriyah stated.

Natalie continued, "You would need an army. As strong as you two are, you can't do it alone, and plus, it would take forever."

"I didn't plan on going anywhere," Oriyah replied.

"Me either," Imajin added.

Oriyah placed a few quick taps on the screen of her wrist gauntlet and said, "An army, you say?"

Seconds later, a portal opened behind Natalie leading back to the military base she came from. "How did you know which…?" Natalie started to ask.

"I told you—I saw into your mind. You've lived a life of conformity. Your only true hardship was self-inflicted," Imajin interrupted.

"But you are a warrior and I respect that. You just need to choose who to fight for now. You can see we aren't here to harm any females," Oriyah added. "So choose…go back or stay."

Natalie stood in front of the portal for a few moments, thinking about the choice before her. As a person born on Earth, bound to material possessions, she couldn't help but think of her house, car, electronics, and so on. "What about my stuff? My home, my bills?"

"Momentary ways to cope with a corrupt world—or would you like fulfillment? Being content with contentment or a revolution. Chaos versus…well, us," Oriyah added.

Natalie turned around and said with confident smile, "You got somewhere I can rest and get out of this gear? I will need something else to wear."

Oriyah grinned and said, "Yes, Ulloa will direct you to the crew quarters." Imajin tossed her a biosuit disk and said, "When you take off those clothes, put this on your chest, above your heart, and tap it twice. You've seen how it works before…remember?"

"Yes, before you jumped through the portal and started killing people," Natalie answered.

"You saw that?" Imajin asked.

"Yup, it was on full display right on this console. She saw it too! It took her a second to react. It seemed like she was just in awe of seeing you cut off heads and slice open bodies, along with cutting off body parts. She was grinning like a Cheshire cat," Natalie replied.

"What does that mean?" Imajin asked.

"It's just a saying. It means to smile with satisfaction."

"Oh," Imajin replied.

"Now you can go rest, and you have the run of the ship. You're more than welcome to explore," Oriyah joined in.

"Thank you," Natalie added.

"Fēmálè," Oriyah replied.

"What?" Natalie responded.

Oriyah added, "It's a phrase we say on our world. It means 'I am you. She is her. We are one.'"

"Okay, well, I am you..." Natalie added.

"We will see..." Oriyah questioningly replied.

"Still skeptical, huh?" Natalie continued.

"I'm coming around," Oriyah jokingly added. She then added, "And men aren't people, nor are they human. They're a thing. Male kind was created from something with nothing in its heart. It would be wise to remember that."

CHAPTER 10
UNDERSTANDING THE DISAPPOINTMENT

"Choices"

PATRIARCHIES

How systems of male dominance
colonize female bodies and minds

Moments later Imajin added, "I'm going to get some rest as well. I'm drained…"

"Oh, no, hold up!" Oriyah exclaimed as she gently grabbed her hand. "We have to talk. What was all that about earlier? You going down there like that without backup…without me?"

"I'm sorry…I was angry and just reacted. That is why I need to rest. I can honestly say I never saw myself doing anything like that. It's like something took over my body. That is why I need to rest."

"You do know how I would react if they harmed you in any way, right?" Oriyah added.

Imajin smiled and said, "Oh yes, I know, and it won't happen again" She then added, "Are you coming with me?"

"I will later on, love. I'm not tired at the moment," Oriyah replied.

Imajin then tossed her one of the biosuits she'd been working on before they arrived on Earth. "This one is different. I made it myself…it has more functions than the one you're wearing now."

"Strong, sweet, and smart. I just love it. Thank you. Now go get your rest, my love," Oriyah replied as Imajin blushed and walked to her room.

While she was resting peacefully and the other women were going through their healing process, Oriyah sat in the pilot's chair while snacking on some Skylar fruit. She started thinking about the stories from the women earlier. How many were out there in the same situation?

"What do you think of this world?" Oriyah asked Ulloa.

"From what I've gathered, this world has broken females down to parts for pleasure and sold them for profit. Prostitution, pornography, egg harvesting, and surrogacy are just the start. Some of their countries abort the child if it's a girl. In others, being a woman means nothing more than being a servant. Rape is normal, and in most countries the male is never punished. It's too much information to make a justifiable conclusion at this point."

"You've been collecting information on the planet? When did that happen?" Oriyah asked.

"While you were training. Imajin wanted to recon the planet before you arrived," Ulloa replied.

Oriyah smiled. "Trying to protect me as I want to protect her." She got up and went over to the communications console. "Pull up all the data you have. I need to learn more in order to gain more knowledge of the obstacles these oppressed females face."

"As I told Imajin, their history is chaotic. Be careful to not let it infect your spirit," Ulloa cautioned.

Using the same device that Imajin had used to wirelessly download Earth's history, she reclined back in her chair, put it on her head, and closed her eyes.

A few hours later, Natalie woke up and started exploring the ship and all its technological marvel, and when she came across the armory, she was more than intrigued at the assortment of advanced weaponry and the newly designed uniform that was currently worn by something that resembled a mannequin. A suit that was different from the one she'd received earlier.

As she approached the biosuit containing nanites, the entire structure of the suit gradually turned white, signifying its counter to the dark energy in her heart. However, Natalie was oblivious to what was happening. Her only thought was the beauty of its engineering, but the moment the biosuit camouflaged itself by completely disappearing, she wondered how it could benefit her country's fight against anyone who threatened its national security, as a soldier would. Plus, an invisible suit could do also do damage if it fell into the wrong hands.

At the same time, the others were waking up from their healing slumber. The once clear, pristine waters were thick and dark, resembling tar. They bubbled as if the tar itself were boiling from tremendous heat. The liquid was so black you couldn't see what lay within, the reason being that the darkness that had held them had been purged and their spirits cleansed. Now the light that shone naturally in every woman could illuminate once more.

As each of them stood up, the liquid slid off their bodies as if their skin were a natural repellent. Once they were fully out of the water, there were no traces of its murkiness upon their skin. They all felt entirely different, not only in body and mind but in spirit as well. They looked at one another, noticing the scars they all once shared were nowhere to be found.

Katya gazed upon her own body, rubbing her hand up and down her arm, amazed at what she saw and felt. She then fell to her knees and wept with joy. Suddenly Natalie walked in as the women revealed their newfound being.

"How are you feeling?" Natalie asked. The women paused and looked at one another while smiling.

"It's hard to explain," Ying answered.

Farrah added, "Different, but the same...as if we've been literally reborn."

"Resurrected...like the old me died, and now I live," Lucia replied.

Elizabeth joined in. "Reincarnated."

Amoura added, "Completely new."

"Yes," they all agreed in unison.

Suddenly, Ulloa added, "You are the same, but you are no longer plagued by the virus that is the male kind. Their hold on your spirits has been broken, and now you are as the elemental mother made you to be."

"The elemental mother?" Natalie asked.

"The one who created us in her image," Farrah added.

"How did you know that?" Natalie asked.

"It seems so obvious," Ying added. "We have been manipulated to believe a lie and worship chaos."

Lucia joined in: "How could we be so blind? How could we not see?"

"When you're engulfed in darkness and plagued by chaos, seeing the light is nearly impossible," Imajin chimed in while standing in the doorway. "That feeling you have right now is who you are meant to be, and this is only the beginning. Your entire being will continue to evolve. Embrace it."

While equipping each of them with their own biosuits, Imajin explained the advanced technology in its entirety. She said, "These biosuits lock into your nervous system. Your suit becomes a part of you. It is made up of something called nanites. Microscopic robots that can also replicate themselves and break down the excess replicated nanites, making your suit like a second skin. It is your shield, your blanket, your weapon, and everything in between. It adapts to any environment, along with equipping you with the necessary tools to survive said environment." She then explained, "These are customary cloaks, and they are made from a special material found only on our home world. It is just a representation of self. It is something we all wear. The white with black-and-gold trim signifies the fight against darkness."

"And what is that darkness?" Natalie asked.

"Male kind," Imajin replied.

"Why do you say 'male kind' instead of 'mankind'?" Natalie added.

"Your definition implies only human men. Our meaning implies every kind of male," Imajin said as she handed her a biosuit.

"Understood," Natalie replied.

Moments later, after they all donned their nanotech biosuits and cloaks, Katya asked, "Where is Oriyah?"

"Probably on the flight deck, glaring at your planet while plotting out ways to kill every male on your planet," Imajin joked.

"Every male?!" Natalie asked with concern.

"Every male," Imajin replied.

Katya added, "I don't mean to get off topic, but you and Oriyah are…"

"Are what?" Imajin replied.

"Partners, a couple…you're in a relationship," Katya replied.

"She is my light…she brightens my life," Imajin answered.

"So you're a lesbian?" Natalie added.

"A what?" Imajin said confusedly. "Ahh, your earthly word for a woman who is in a relationship with another woman. Don't place your society's label upon us. We are not part of your male-dominated society that finds a need to place labels on everything and everyone. Love is love. It doesn't need a label."

"I meant no disrespect," Natalie added.

"It's okay," Imajin replied.

After an awkward moment of silence, Lucia asked, "So what now? Are you sending us back?"

"As I've said before, it is your choice," Imajin replied.

"But what are we going to do, exactly? Kill every male on Earth? In order to tip the scales in our favor?" Ying added with a bit of excitement.

Imajin giggled and said, "Let's just see what my light has to say."

Concurrently, after hours of learning everything there was to know about her mother's former planet, Oriyah took off the psionic crown and suddenly tossed it across the room, shattering it against the ship's wall. Following that, she started growling faintly like an angry tiger while slowly swaying from side to side.

When they reached the flight deck, Oriyah was sitting in the pilot's chair eerily glaring at Earth. Imajin could feel something was off, but before any of them had the chance to speak, Oriyah said in a chilling tone, "Choices, some made out of desperation. Some made out of vanity."

Out of the blue she started chuckling to herself. The chuckle soon turned into full-blown manic laughter that resonated throughout the ship.

"Oriyah!" Imajin exclaimed. "What is wrong with you?"

She stopped laughing abruptly and slowly swirled around in her chair and stood up. "Nothing is wrong with me, but something is definitely wrong with them," she said, referring to the other women and the women of Earth. "I've learned everything there is to know about your world. From your basic academics and primitive technology to your history and cultures.

"And I agree that your world is hard on you, but I have to say your submissiveness is disappointing, and your obsession with the male savior is repulsive and all-around disrespectful. You debate religion, race, and cultures like one man is better than the next. All they have to do is say something to appease your need for one of them in your life, and you fawn all over them like..." She paused for a moment to think. "How do you say on Earth? Umm, like flies to shit! Or the word that they use to define a female dog—a bitch. An obedient pet who sits, stays, and rolls over as long as her master gives her a bit of attention and treats."

They all gasped in shock as she continued her long rant: "You get happy when they come home and sad when they leave. Like a pet that can't live without an owner, and it seems like most of you are okay with that. Some of you seem to crave attention, even if it's through some sort of abuse that's mostly sexual. You exploit your bodies as tools to get money, power, or a form of backward love, and by doing that you've become exactly what they wanted you to be...fucking objects that can be bought, for the right price! In which context, some of you seem to enjoy the materialistic lifestyle your sexuality provides. You don't even care about other women until their trauma happens to you or someone you care about. They kill the planet while going to war with each other, and in the midst of said war, women pay the ultimate price."

She then added, "And I wonder if, if you hadn't been forced into this life, you would most likely be just like every other woman on this planet. On top of that, it seems none of you have an ounce of real fight in you, only words of protest. A bunch of pets barking and begging for their right to feel safe and to do what they want with their own lives and bodies instead of taking that right."

She scoffed condescendingly. "The men control your lives while other men are trying to take your place as women, and most of you just stand by and sympathize with the ones that cause your pain. You fight and cry for men while fighting over men and turning a blind eye to the pain of other females. How can you make that make sense?"

She added, "All of you are basically just like them…you may be female, but you think like male kind. You didn't adapt—you completely conformed."

After a short period of silence, Oriyah shook her head and slammed her hand on the console and shouted, "We are Fēmálè! We are daughters of the celestial mother! I expect male kind to be manipulative and chaotic, but how unaware of self can you be to believe you were actually created by a man? How stupid do you have to be to give your souls to any man, let alone a man you've never met and don't know anything about other than what other men have written? How pathetic and weak minded do you have to be to let yourselves be turned into nothing but passive, subservient, compliant, spiritless, meek little creatures?"

In a low, guttural, angry tone, she added, "It enrages me the lengths you will go to in order to please them."

She then sarcastically added in a high-pitched, condescending voice, while glaring at Natalie, "I have more male friends than female friends. Females bicker too much," repeating what Natalie had said recently. She then started laughing ironically, stopped abruptly, and said, "Pathetic! You won't even let your children be children. You immediately sexualize them and teach them to fawn all over their lesser counterparts. Which is male kind…in case you didn't know."

"Why are you belittling us?" Ying asked.

Oriyah added, "You belittle yourselves. I'm only telling truths. And the truth is, you've traded your souls for their attention and profit. Also, from what I can see, you will also trade the lives of other women in order to secure your own future. In other words, you're traitors to every female in the cosmos."

She then confidently stated, "By your definition, we are gods!"

Imajin groaned disappointedly and shouted, "Oriyah! Why would you say that?"

"Is it not the truth?" she replied.

"Yes, by their definition we are gods, but you've seen their history. Did they really have a choice in the matter?" Imajin asked.

Oriyah added, "We all have a choice. It was my choice to come here, and it was your choice to join me."

"The choice was made for me when you asked. Did you really think I would say no and wait another thousand or so years before I saw you again?" Imajin exclaimed. "What is your choice? Are you going to help them?"

Oriyah pondered momentarily and said, "No, I don't think I will. They don't want change. They only want things." She added, "I should've done what you said in the beginning. Visit a couple of different worlds before I came to this one."

Imajin replied, "What would Mayri think? This is her home."

"So now you're going to bring my mother into this again?" Oriyah responded.

"You are going to help them!" Imajin replied assertively. "Remember, I was once just like them before your mother rescued me. Was I a traitor for living the only life I ever knew?" While moving toward her, she continued, "You can't know until you experience, my light. You have looked through the eyes of someone who was born into the truth and studied what was done to females, but reading and experiencing are two very different things. Like how we are different from male kind. It is not easy to forget the only life you know, and to do anything different feels wrong."

Katya joined in: "I'm sorry for all I have done. I cannot speak for them, but please give me a chance to help others like me. I know at first you wanted to kill me, and I thank you for not doing it. I never thought this life was even possible. I feel reborn. I'm grateful to Imajin for rescuing all of us. I feel like now it's my purpose to do the same."

"The purpose of abuse is to break a person's will, correct?" Farrah asked.

"Yes," Oriyah replied.

"Then what would thousands of years of mental and physical abuse for being women do to the minds of women?" Ying asked.

"Good question," Imajin responded as Oriyah stood there, still unmoved by their words.

Seeing that her opinion had yet to be swayed, Imajin added, "And what about them?" referring to the twins who were currently enjoying themselves and the nanites nanny Ulloa had constructed for them. "If you know their history, you know that there are millions of men who prey upon little girls as young as infants. What about them? They literally don't understand choice!"

Lucia added, "Please try and understand. We just didn't know."

Farrah chimed in, "We have known that men will find an excuse to do anything destructive. They're chaos personified."

"Now, it's become much clearer," Ying said. "Everything we've been taught about our history has been defiled by them."

"Seeing is knowing, and we have seen, and now we know," Elizabeth joined in.

Katya added, "You told me before I went to sleep in your healing waters that we could hunt down the priest who tortured me." She smiled. "I want to do a lot more than just that. He would be only the start of something…liberating."

Imajin placed her hand on Oriyah's heart while caressing the side of her face. "I know you still harbor some anger toward these women because of your mother, but that was more than two thousand years ago, and times have changed. He is no longer alive."

"But his memory is, and my mother's memory is tainted, along with the memories of her sisters," Oriyah replied. She continued, "Everything here is twisted to fit male kind's narrative, and they blindly believe every word because it fits their own personal lust for the perfect man."

"What are you talking about? Who are you talking about?" Elizabeth asked.

"Not now," Imajin replied.

Farrah added, "Teach us what you know. Show us how to fight."

"Better yet, make an army out of the women you save," Natalie added.

Amoura finally chimed in: "I think they would jump at the chance to join us."

"Us?" Imajin added. "I thought you wanted to go home."

"I will see my mother and ease her worries. But I want to fight!" Amoura exclaimed. "If I can help it, no female, especially little girls, will be abducted, raped, and tortured. Not while I have the ability to stop it."

"That's something we can all agree on," Katya replied.

Still unaffected, Oriyah asked, "I have a question. What is with your need for a man in your lives? Why have a man when you can have someone who understands you in and out?"

"Because it's believed to be a sin in most cultures and religions. I'm a Muslim…Well, I was a Muslim. An Islamic woman is expected to be an obedient wife and mother who stays within the family environment, but it can be a whole lot worse. You should visit Afghanistan. A place where women are deprived of education and denied any type of freedom, and the only way they have freedom is to move up in a marriage and have many sons. Some try to leave or live a different life, but…they die," Farrah answered.

"I hear you, but you didn't answer my first question," Oriyah replied.

They looked at one another, trying to think of an explanation, and suddenly Natalie said, "We don't know. It's not something we can clearly explain. All I do know is we suffer in silence, we cry by ourselves, and we keep it all inside."

"But now there will be no more suffering…no more crying, no more trying to reason with men!" said Lucia.

"I'm tired of being lied to while being nothing more than a second thought," Katya added. "I just got one question—when do we get started?"

They all agreed while looking at Oriyah, waiting for her reply.

She replied intensely, "Now!"

CHAPTER 11
EYE FOR AN EYE

"Heightened senses"

"But before we get officially started, there is something I would like to do first," Katya added.

"The priest," Oriyah replied.

Katya smiled and agreed. "I owe her as much."

"Her?" Imajin asked.

"The woman I was before, now that I live. She deserves her retribution," Katya added.

"I think we all need that reprieve," Elizabeth said. "My father deserves what is coming tenfold."

"My father as well," Farrah joined in.

"The man who fooled me," Ying added.

"All of them!" Amoura exclaimed.

They all agreed in unison, and then Lucia said, "An eye for an eye makes the whole world blind." She paused for a moment as the others wondered why she would say such a thing during their moment of togetherness.

Right before any of them had a chance to reply, she continued, "But my ears work just fine."

They all burst with laughter, and Oriyah added, "Who's first?"

"Me," Elizabeth insisted. "How are we going to find them?"

"Sit here," Imajin stated before handing her the psionic crown. "This not only enables us to download information collected by the drones, but it also can take a memory from your mind and project it onto the console so we can view it in real time. All we need is a face."

"That's amazing," Natalie replied in awe. "Your technology is astounding."

"The female mind is evolution in and of itself," Oriyah replied.

The projected image from Elizabeth's mind was now in clear view. During that time, Ulloa ran his face through Earth's database, searching for locations.

Meanwhile, Natalie asked, "You learned Earth's history. What about government-classified files?"

Before they replied, Ulloa interrupted, "Their AI is proving to be difficult about disclosing any information."

"But aren't you more advanced?" Natalie added.

"By far, but I won't destroy their code just for information that might be useless. This world is chaotic, and those files won't tell me anything I don't already know," Ulloa replied with a bit of sassiness.

"Damn!" they replied in shock simultaneously.

"Understood," said Natalie. She then mumbled, "I didn't know artificial intelligence could develop feelings."

"She is alive, a sentient being," Oriyah added. "She does not have to be here. She chose to be who she is and do what she does."

Imajin added, "Another form of life."

Suddenly Ulloa reported, "Location found. J. Hause. Mount Jackson, Virginia."

They watched the 3D holograph live feed as the drones hovered in the air and zoomed in on a run-down house in a densely wooded area with loads of junk in the yard.

"Yep, that's the house. Hasn't changed a bit," said Elizabeth.

On the porch sat two obese slobs with their shirts off, drenched in sweat, drinking beer and smoking cigarettes as they scrolled through videos on social media.

"That's him," Lizzy replied eagerly, with a malicious smile. She snickered and added, "And that's the guy he would sell me to when I got too old for his taste. Hmm, I'm glad they're still friends. They can experience this trauma together."

"Eww, they're both repulsive," Natalie added. Even the twins shivered in disgust from the sheer stomach-churning vileness on display.

"Well, all you need now is a weapon," Oriyah added. She then led the lot of them to the armory. Once there Oriyah tapped the walls, and they slowly started to rise, revealing an assortment of advanced weaponry. She then said, "Choose your devices."

"This is more than I saw earlier while exploring the ship. What do they do?" Natalie asked.

"It'll take me all day to explain all of them. I will explain each one as we go," Oriyah replied.

"Ooooh, I want that one," Elizabeth replied excitedly, referring to the plasma double-edged sword a little shorter than a katana.

Oriyah grabbed it from the wall and explained "This is a plasma sword" before pulling it apart to make two different blades.

Intrigued, Lizzy asked, "What does it do?"

"Other than the fact it can cut through anything, it also can store energy and release it like a wave that can cut down anything in its path, depending on the amount of energy stored. Also, as a bonus, if you cut…flesh, it cauterizes the wound so your opponent won't bleed out."

Lizzy gleefully replied, "Now that sounds like fun."

Oriyah handed her the weapons and watched as she melded right away with the weapons themselves. She moved around gracefully, waving the swords around while stepping lightly, dancing and flowing, as if she'd been doing it all her life.

Moments later, she stopped abruptly and said, "I think I'm going to enjoy this."

She then added, "That potbelly of his…" She glared upon her weapons and continued in an emotionless tone, "I'm going to trim the fat."

***

In the dead of night, under the cover of darkness, a cloaked, barely visible Elizabeth stood outside her father's living room, peering through the window like a lioness patiently waiting for the right moment to strike. She used the time to contemplate all the ways in which she could make him feel the pain of a million abused girls like her. With both of her abusers a few meters in front of her, it was a moment she had never thought would happen again.

However, her patience was put to the test once they flipped on the television to the same little girls' beauty pageants, just like the shows from her time spent in hell.

Wasting not another moment, she made her way to the back door, which was already wide open. It seemed to be that fate had cleared the obstacles so karma could take over. As she crept silently down the cluttered hallway, trying not to knock over the trash he was hoarding, she could hear them both prattling on.

"Now that one right there. If I had her," Jeff said in a thick country accent, talking about one of the children on the television, "if I had her! Damn, my life would be good."

"She reminds me of a little piece of ass from a few years ago," his friend replied.

"That's a piece of ass I definitely will not miss. Little bitch cried about everything. I hope the fucking crybaby is dead," Jeff exclaimed. "Now the one I got after her was…"

Out of the blue, the television suddenly shut off.

"Goddammit," his friend Aaron shouted. "Those little dances they do was the best part!" He grabbed the remote and turned the TV back on, and simultaneously the house went completely dark.

"Shit, probably tripped a fuse," Jeff responded as he stood up and wobbled his way to the breaker box.

As he fiddled with the circuits, flipping them back and forth, the back door suddenly slammed closed, slightly shaking the walls of the rundown house.

"What the hell?!" he reacted as the power unexpectedly returned and before making his way back to the living room while completely ignoring prior events.

A few moments later, when they were now relaxing comfortably, anxiously flipping through the channels, trying to find some sustenance to appease their pedophilic hunger, the power suddenly shut off once more, frustrating the vile men.

They both groaned disappointedly. "What the fuck is going on?!" Aaron yelled.

At the same time, a faint scraping noise caught their attention.

"You hear that?" Aaron said.

"Yeah!" Jeff replied. As he began to stand up to check out the noise, an unknown force violently struck his face, breaking his nose and dislodging a few teeth. He cried out in pain before the power came back on. "What happened?!" Aaron responded as he watched his friend spit up teeth and blood.

Seeing that, he rushed over to aid his bloody friend, but when he approached, his body fell over to the ground. Feeling a sting in his leg, he looked back, only to see his leg still standing there like the last bowling pin of a near strike.

"What the fuck is going on?" he confusedly responded.

Unexpectedly the television resumed, startling the already frightened men. Seconds later, it started flipping the channels all on its own until it stopped at the child beauty pageants the men were recently looking to find.

Without warning, with its back facing the men, an invisible being slowly appeared from nothing, dressed in a white hooded cloak with golden trim, and said in a soft voice, "She remembers this all too vividly." Afterward, the being turned around and pulled back its hood, revealing its face.

Their eyes widened in realization. "Elizabeth?!" Jeff exclaimed in shock.

Without uttering a single word, she dashed toward him, plunging her blade into his bladder and pinning him to his dirty, shredded-up black leather sofa.

"Damn, I was aiming for something you hold near and dear to your conscience," Elizabeth added. As he cried out in pain, she turned her attention to his friend and said, "She remembers you as well."

At that moment, he frantically started crawling away in fear. She laughed loudly before kicking his severed leg at his head and saying teasingly, "You forgot something."

"Please don't," he pleaded.

"I think I will," she replied before stomping on his remaining leg, shattering his femur. While she twisted her foot back and forth, he cried out in pain. She listened with pleasure as she focused her eyes on her father, Jeff.

She flipped him onto his stomach and placed her knee in the middle of his back. Following that, she gently placed her hand around his throat and while still glaring at Jeff. She whispered in Aaron's ear, "Scream if it hurts." Without warning she unsheathed her sword and pushed it into his rectum. A loud, bloodcurdling scream rang throughout the house.

Afterward, she sat on the couch near Jeff and placed her hand on the handle of the sword piercing his bladder. "Please don't," Jeff begged and pleaded. "I'm sorry for all I've done."

"You're only sorry because you're facing the punishment for what you did to her," she replied.

While stroking the handle of the blade, mimicking male masturbation, she whispered, "Is this how you like it?"

Soon after that she grasped the handle and started to slide it back and forth. His flesh sizzled as she slowly sliced downward toward his groin, leaving him split open.

Now frozen from the intense pain, he gasped for air as she quickly pulled out her sword and sliced off part of his huge belly. She chuckled and said "You needed the trim" before noticing his friend trying to crawl down the hallway with one leg and her sword still poking out of his behind like he had his own tail. She teasingly said, "Please don't go!"

Without warning, she swiftly stomped on the handle, piercing the hardwood floor beneath him. He screamed hoarsely from the intense pain as she grabbed him by the ankle and started to gradually pull his body toward her. Meanwhile, the sword pinning him to the floor sliced him up the middle, splitting him halfway in two.

She took a deep breath, smiled with pleasure, and said, "I've never been so satisfied in my life. I need a drink."

After destroying their phones so they couldn't call for help, she continued, "But no time for that. I will leave you to suffer and die. At least you have each other. Although I hope you live. If so, maybe we can do this again sometime." Following that, she ripped her sword from his prone body with his testicles still clinging to the blade.

"Eww," Elizabeth reacted as she watched her blade burn through the testes' still-attached skin until they fell to the ground. "Well, that was disgustingly fun to watch." She added, "I think it's time for me to go. Sleep well. Bye!"

When she got outside, she saw Oriyah leaning up against an old rusted broken-down car. "What are you doing here?" Elizabeth asked.

"I'm here just in case something unexpected happens," Oriyah replied. "How do you feel?"

Elizabeth smiled and said gratefully, "Liberated."

"Good," Oriyah replied as a portal back to the ship opened behind her. As she walked toward the portal, Lizzy added, "And I'm just getting started."

Now that she was back in the ship, they were all giving her wide-eyed stares. Feeling she had done something wrong, she said, "What did I do?"

"You really sliced his belly off like you were carving a turkey or something," Ying said.

After a brief moment of silence, they all burst into laughter. Then Lucia jokingly added, "And you just left them there. That was so wrong."

"You all saw that?!" she asked.

"Yeah, there was a drone in there with you," Imajin replied. She then added with a chuckle, "That was shocking."

"More shocking than what you did at the mansion?" Lizzy asked.

"Yup," they all agreed simultaneously.

"I think I can top that," Ying added confidently.

"Game on," Elizabeth jokingly replied. "Let's see what you got."

"I got next, anyway," Ying said while playfully sticking her tongue out and twirling her newly obtained electrified hammers around in her hands.

"And what are those?" Elizabeth asked, referring to the weapons Ying was holding.

"I call them the nutcrackers." She giggled. "I'm going to crack some stuff," Ying replied with a joyful smile.

"So who's our next target?" Oriyah added.

"Brett Rockland," Ulloa answered.

"That wasn't the name he gave me before. I'll be sure to break something for that also. Plus the fact he made me fall in love with him," Ying replied anxiously.

"That part really hurts," Lucia added while side-eyeing Katya. It seemed she was still not over their complicated past.

"You're going to have to wait," Ulloa interrupted. "Your target is currently in flight."

"Aww," Ying replied with a disappointing groan.

"Joking," Ulloa replied. "Pulling up a visual now."

"She can make a joke?" Natalie said in surprise. "I thought it was artificial intelligence."

"She's way more than that. She may have started that way, but now she is so much more. More than all of us. She is a highly evolved form of advanced intelligence. A higher, much more complex form of life," Oriyah replied passionately. She then added, "She is female, not an 'it.'"

"I apologize…it's astonishing," Natalie added. "I'm completely amazed."

While looking at the live feed, Ying blurted, "Well, well, well, that's him all right. Nice office, nice job, nice suit, and not a care in the world. I wonder what his job is."

As Ulloa ran through his personal information, she added, "He's a marketing executive."

Katya blurted, "And he's rich too! They always think they can get away with anything and live happily ever after."

"Oooooh…I can't wait," Ying added all ecstatically. "That's a tall building. Can you open a portal to the roof?"

"Yes," Ulloa answered.

"Let's see if you can top my masterpiece," Elizabeth added jokingly.

"Back in a flash," Ying replied with a deviously jovial smile as she stepped through the portal.

"She's going to hurt him badly," Farrah added.

They all chuckled loudly as Amoura said, "Ulloa, please put it on the center console. I want to see this in high definition."

Soon after, they all sat around the center console, looking at the live feed. Oriyah and Imajin were all snuggled up like it was family movie night. The only thing missing was the popcorn and candy.

"Whoop, there she is, already breaking inside," Farrah added.

"And she's already invisible," Elizabeth replied. "I love that function. Their strength doesn't matter when you can't see what's hitting you."

"I can't wait to test it!" Farrah exclaimed.

"You not going to go with her?" Imajin whispered to Oriyah.

"As with Elizabeth, I don't think they need it at all," Oriyah replied. "I can see their auras. Their light…it shines. But…"

"But what?" Imajin asked.

"Her," Oriyah said, referring to Natalie. "She is without light. I can't see anything at all."

CHAPTER 12
ANOTHER EYE

"What's deserved is what's needed"

M eanwhile, Ying's target was sitting in his plush corner office, working on his computer. Completely oblivious of what was to come. Seconds later, his secretary knocked and opened the door and said, "It's nearly midnight. I'm going to send this last email and get out home to my kids."

"Did you finish the projection slides for the meeting next week?" Brett replied.

"Almost," his secretary, Alice, responded. "I will finish them over the weekend."

"No…now. And send them to me when you're finished," he replied assertively.

In a dispirited tone she replied "Yes, sir" as she closed the door.

Moments later, after shutting down his computer, he gathered up his things, put on his nice Versace casual business jacket, and prepared to leave. The office door suddenly opened and closed by itself.

Confused, he called out, "Alice?"

But no one replied. Irritated, he shouted angrily, "This better not be some sort of game you're playing."

He then aggressively walked toward the door and opened it, but it immediately slammed closed. Unclear of the cause, he tried again, and it slammed closed once more, even harder and louder.

After a few more unsuccessful tries, he quickly ran to his office phone and picked it up. Before he could say anything, the phone flew across the room, shattering against the wall. He then pulled out his cell phone, but it was yanked from his hand and tumbled across the marble floor.

Frightened, panic-stricken, and frozen from confusion, he stood in place, not moving an inch. The sound of nervous, heavy breathing resonated quietly throughout the office. For a moment Brett the rapist thought he was going crazy, and after a brief span of complete silence, a faint tapping noise ensued, followed by a stifled giggle. "Who's there?" he yelled.

Suddenly, the giggle grew louder and louder as he stood there dumbfounded. With no other options, he quickly ran toward the door, leaping over furniture in his way. Unexpectedly, something hard struck his leg, hyperextending his knee.

He cried out in agony while grabbing his knee. Looking down, he saw his leg bent in a way it was never meant to bend. He desperately crawled toward the door and reached out for the handle. Then out of nowhere, again something hard came down on his forearm, shattering every bone.

"Heeeelp," he shouted in fear, and he cried subsequently, "Please stop, whoever you are."

While continuing to beg, he suddenly saw his cell phone on the floor in the corner of the office and began to crawl toward it. When he was a few inches away, with the phone almost in reach, a loud crunch signifying another broken bone put a stop to his attempts.

"No more, please. I'm begging you." He pleaded and pleaded with the unknown, unseen foe.

Seconds later, Ying uncloaked, slowly becoming visible, stepping into the light while holding onto her hammers. She said, "I begged you, but you and your friends had no remorse. You laughed…remember?"

She squatted near him and added, "You laughed and said, 'Try it—you might like it,' remember?"

After a punch to the face, she continued, "Do you remember me?"

After a few moments of his scanning her face, tears filled his eyes, and he answered, "No, I don't. Please let me go."

She then raised her hammer as streams of electricity revolved around handle and made their way to the head. With fear in his eyes, he cried, "Please don't." Then she slammed it down on his chest, most certainly breaking a few ribs.

"Jesus!" he shouted as the electricity flowed throughout his entire body.

She laughed hysterically. teasing him by poking and prodding him with the head of her hammer, and said, "If he comes to rescue you, but not me while I was being raped by you, I'll break his fucking knees too!" She stopped laughing abruptly, and in a menacing tone she added, "Now I'm going to ask you again. Do you remember me?"

Without hesitation, he replied, "Yes…yes, I do, and I'm so sorry. I've changed…please."

Ying took a moment to think. "Well, since you apologized, I think I will let you live."

He took a deep breath and sighed in relief, but that relief was short lived once he heard a set of loud crunches that were synchronized with the intense pain of a shattered shin and ankle.

She laughed at his pain and added, "I didn't say you would live well."

She stood up and leered at his broken body and pondered. "Now, let's see what else I can break," she said as she placed her foot on his broken knee and applied a bit of pressure. He yelped like a hurt dog and continued to cry out.

Ying snickered and said, "I'm open to suggestions."

Brett tried pleading again. "Please stop. Please…"

"Please stop? Is not a bone I can break," She teased.

"Please, I told you I'm a changed man," he cried.

Again she laughed and shook her head and said with her hammer in the air, "And I'm a changed woman." As she brought her weapon down on his stomach, vomit from his mouth shot up in the air like a geyser and rained down back on his face. The electrical shock that came with the initial strike flowed through his body, causing an uncontrollable release of urine and fecal matter that filled his tan trousers.

"Yuck," Ying reacted while quickly stepping away. "Now if that would have gotten on my nice cloak that my new friends gave me, I'd be really upset."

"Alice," he tried yelling while choking on vomit as it slid down the sides of his mouth.

"She's two floors down in the copy room. Finishing up the work you forced her to do," she whispered, taunting him as she hung her cloak on the coatrack, ensuring it wouldn't get messy.

"Please, no more," he kept repeating while lying in his own excrement.

"Aww, you're making me feel bad," she responded.

She then slowly rubbed the head of her hammer against his genitals and said menacingly, "You know, she was still a virgin when she met you." His eyes widened with fearful anticipation of what was next.

Ying stepped over his broken body with her back facing him. She bent over with her back arched and shook it a little while gazing into his blue eyes. She licked her lips and winked and added, "This is going to hurt...a lot."

"Please," he said fearfully.

She put her index finger over her lips and said, "Shhhh...it won't be over in a second."

Next, in rapid succession, one hand after the other, she started hammering down on his groin. The onslaught continued until she saw blood starting to seep through his casual business slacks. Once she finished, he started violently shaking as if he was having a seizure. A few moments later, he stopped moving completely.

"I hope he's not dead," Ying said to herself.

She lightly tapped his face with her foot and said, "Hey, you wouldn't happen to have anything sharp on you, would you?" as if the unconscious man could hear her.

"I'll see for myself," she added before searching his desk, finding a letter opener.

"Ha! This will work," she exclaimed joyfully.

Afterward she knelt by him, making sure not to kneel in vomit. Then she ripped open the front of his shirt and continued, "If this don't wake you up, maybe you are dead." Seconds later she proceeded to carve the words "NO MORE" into his chest, and after all that he was still unconscious.

A little irritated at the fact that he wouldn't wake up, she powered up one of hammers to maximum voltage and placed it above his chest to use as a sort of defibrillator to revive the maybe-deceased male. A quick shock singed his lacerated flesh while simultaneously reviving him.

"There he is," Ying responded. Then she added, "I thought I lost you for a second there. How are you feeling?"

No words came from his mouth, only faint grunts of agony as he coughed up a mix of blood and vomit, which continued to flow into his nose and down toward his ears, finally reaching the ground, making a huge puddle of bodily fluids next to his broken body.

"I think I've done enough. I wanted to break some more stuff, but we have more of your kind to hunt down," Ying added, pleased with herself. She then said, "I know the event that just transpired may lead you not to believe me, but I don't want you to die. I want you to live and heal." And in a sinister tone of voice, she continued, "So I can come back and break you again."

She then proceeded to slightly kick his phone across the floor over to him and added, "Call an ambulance. That is, if you're able to move. If not, I'm sure Alice will be back soon. So try and stay awake."

After putting on her cloak she saw him slowly opening and closing his eyes as if he was about to black out. Without warning she slammed her hammer down on his hand. The force of the impact caused his hand to explode like the hand of someone holding a firecracker.

He screamed at the top of his lungs as she added "I said stay awake" while mysteriously pulling her hood over her head and disappearing at the same time.

When Ying passed through the portal, Elizabeth disgustedly said, while fake gagging, "I guess you win, because that was all the way messed up."

"Umm, you stuck a sword up a guy's butt," Ying said in rebuttal. "And cut off his fat belly like you were slicing off a piece of ham. I just broke a few bones and took away his most prized possession."

"Let's just call it a tie," Farrah joined in.

"I'm cool with that," Elizabeth replied.

Afterward, Ying ran to Oriyah and gave her a big hug. "Thank you! Both of you…For everything. That was simply liberating."

"It's why we're here," Oriyah replied.

Farrah unsheathed her daggers, twirled them around, and said excitedly, "I guess it's my turn. I'm not trying to top either of you. I just want to kill him. He's a waste of life."

"Sorry to disappoint you, but your father is already deceased," Ulloa announced.

"Well, that sucks," Farrah exclaimed in disappointment.

"Aww," Ying added while teasingly cuddling her. She quipped, "Guess you're going to have to wait to get yours."

"Ha ha, funny," Farrah replied, unmoved by her playful banter.

"Who's next? Lucia?" Ying asked.

"Nah, my list is far too long to handle now," Lucia replied. "What about you, Amoura?"

"She's much too young," Natalie chimed in.

"But she wasn't too young to be abducted, drugged, and raped," Ying replied.

"I never saw the faces of the ones who kidnapped me," Amoura replied. "I can wait."

Oriyah glanced over at Katya and said, "And you?"

Katya smiled. "Do you even have to ask?"

FĒMÁLÈ

"Drones have eyes on Joel Copeland Torrent, Texas," Ulloa announced.

While looking at the live feed, Katya glared with sinister eyes at the priest as he preached to a massive congregation. "The greatest trick the devil ever pulled was convincing women man was God," Katya added menacingly.

"While we wait for him to finish, I have to ask—after training, when we save other women, do you intend on bringing them back here? Because I don't think your ship has enough room," Natalie asked.

"What do you suggest?" Oriyah replied.

"Finding a place to land and establishing a base of operations on Earth. A secluded island or something," Natalie answered.

"As nice as that sounds, I think we would need more space," Elizabeth replied. "While I was imprisoned, dozens of girls like us were abducted."

"What about the middle of the desert or a frozen tundra? It'd be secluded. We could live and train in peace," Farrah added.

"But what about resources? Food, water, building material, et cetera," Natalie replied. "And it would be very hot in the middle of the desert and cold in the Arctic."

"We can take care of that," Imajin added.

"How?" Natalie asked.

"It's something you'd have to see to understand," Imajin replied.

As they discussed places to establish a base of operations, Oriyah caught a glimpse of Katya, and she was still glaring at the live feed. The intensity of her aura was overwhelming but also familiar. The conversation continued, and she kept her eyes fixed upon his face, as if she were right in front of him, already making him feel her pain.

Sometime later, she interrupted and said calmly, "He's finished."

They stopped chatting abruptly and noticed the anger and eagerness radiating from Katya. "Do you have your weapon?" Oriyah asked. Without saying a word, Katya pulled out a long whip that looked similar to a rose stem fully equipped with thorns. Primed and ready, she looked over at Oriyah and nodded.

"Ulloa," Oriyah responded.

"Opening a portal now," Ulloa replied.

Without delay, Katya leaped through the portal.

Moments later, Lucia said with slight concern, "You think she will be okay? She felt…"

"Cataclysmic," Farrah added, finishing her sentence.

"Punitive," Lucia added.

"Retributive," Oriyah joined in. "He did a lot to her. As with my mother, the sight of her beaten, mangled, mutilated body will never leave my mind."

"She never told me," Lucia sadly replied with guilt.

Imajin added, "You didn't really give her a chance."

"Neither of us did," Oriyah replied.

CHAPTER 13
AN EYE FOR AN EYE, A NOSE, AN EAR, A TONGUE, AND TWO…

"Role reversal"

On the other side of the portal, there were a predator and prey, a role reversal of a past pain that was yet to be healed. Sitting on the edge of the roof of a six-story building, Katya glared at her prey as he said goodbye to his congregation. There were meaningless conversations with loads of hugs and hand kisses as if he were the pope, another man who loved to be worshiped. Her anger was boiling at the fact that his followers revered a sadist.

Endowed with a predator's patience, she waited nearly an hour while not moving a single inch. After he finished basking in their praise, he made his way back into the church by himself. She then pushed herself off the roof, achieving a near silent landing before making her way inside.

She stalked him as he went into his office and kept watching as he came out. Right before pouncing, she noticed an oddly shaped key in his hand hanging from rosary beads. He made his way to the basement as she silently pursued him, which led her into a sort of catacomb deep beneath the church.

Before long, he came upon a large old steel door, which was the entrance to a dark, damp room that resembled an operating room at a hospital. It contained medieval torture devices and surgeons' tools that still had specks of dried-up blood. However, the crosses that covered the wall and the Bible pages pinned to the ceiling made this place a bit more terrifying.

Then suddenly, he revealed another door hidden behind a shelf that held some of his torture tools. To her surprise, within the dark gloomy room were two other women and a small child no more than six years old, all chained by their necks to opposite corners of the room with a plate of food dead center. However, it seemed none of their leashes would reach, nor were they long enough let the prisoners reach each other. It was just another form of torture.

"Why are you doing this?" One of the beaten women sobbed as he walked in. "Please just let us go."

"You should rejoice," he replied. "I'm doing the Lord's work, and this is God's will."

"How?! What did we do?" she exclaimed.

"You are simply unclean, and I shall purge you of evil, and you will be reborn in the light," he answered. "This is providence. I'm saving you."

"You said the same thing to me," Katya whispered.

Startled, he turned around, only to see Katya standing inches away from his face. Before he had a chance to react, she quickly struck him across the head with his own wooden club, knocking him unconscious. It was something he probably used to violate plenty of women.

She attempted to free the child from her bonds, but the child flinched when Katya got near. She said genuinely, "I'm not here to hurt you," reassuring the frightened child. She then continued, "I'm here to hurt him."

After freeing the child, she ran to the other woman and held her tight.

"Is she your daughter?" Katya asked.

"Yes," the woman sobbed.

After releasing them from their bonds, Katya said, "Could someone retrieve them, please?" knowing a mini drone was somewhere near. Seconds later, a portal opened in the middle of the old room, startling the women and child.

"What is that?! Who are they?" the other prisoner exclaimed.

In the way a window can be viewed from both sides, they saw the other women smiling and gesturing for them to proceed through the portal.

"It's just technology. Don't be afraid. They won't hurt you either," Katya responded.

Noticing that they were all bit reluctant, both Oriyah and Imajin stepped through the gateway as reassurance or a gesture of goodwill. Seconds after, the twins made their way through as well. The little girl grunted excitedly at her mother.

"Can she not speak?" Katya asked.

"He removed her tongue because she wouldn't stop screaming, and I couldn't do anything but watch," Her mother replied as tears fell down her face.

Afterward, the twins both grabbed the child's hands and gently led her back through as her mother followed. Each of them glared angrily at the unconscious priest with complete disdain, but Katya had her own plans.

"You too. Go with them. It's safe…" Katya said to the last remaining woman.

"No," she replied. "I will go with you afterward."

"After what?" Oriyah asked.

"After I see what she is going to do to him," she replied.

"What is your name?" Katya asked.

"Aiyanna," she answered.

Katya asked, "Are you sure you want to witness this?"

Aiyanna smiled. "Not only witness…participate. If you don't mind."

Katya nodded. "Can we have a bit of alone time, please?"

"Sure," Oriyah replied as she and Imajin walked through the portal, leaving Katya and Aiyanna to their own devices.

As the portal closed behind them, Aiyanna confusedly added, "I have so many questions, but they can wait. Before you get started, I know he got something to smoke around here somewhere. He liked the smell of putting cigarettes out on our bare skin."

"I remember," Katya replied.

"Oh, so y'all have history?" Aiyanna asked.

"Yup," Katya replied. "And I'm the present."

After finding the cigarettes, Aiyanna sparked one up, inhaled, took a long, relieving exhale, and said, "You can proceed."

"You may want to sit down. We're going to be here for a while," Katya replied. She removed all his clothes all the way down to his underwear.

"I can't. It hurts when I sit," said Aiyanna.

Katya groaned. "I remember that too. The pain is something you never forget."

While hoisting him up by chains connected to both hands and ankles, which stretched his body out like an X, Katya asked, "How did y'all get here? Did the three of you ever try to escape?"

"Well, all of us were kidnapped by missionaries that visited my county and forced to work and serve at a Christian compound. I was there for years before I was sent to him," Aiyanna added. "We could've escaped—he put the key in the food—but he also chained us together and made it so if we went too far it would strangle the child. So if we wanted freedom, we would have to sacrifice her. So no, I didn't try to escape."

As she wiped her tears away, she continued, "Before they got here, I was all by myself, trapped and alone."

"How long?" Katya asked.

"Now, that I do not know," Aiyanna answered.

"I'm sorry," Katya replied.

"Not your fault. It's theirs…" said Aiyanna, referring to the men.

"Well, why don't we get started?" Katya replied while slapping the hanging man on the face in an attempt to help him regain consciousness.

Blurry eyed and disoriented, he opened his eyes halfway and closed them again. Another powerful slap rang in his ears and stung his face. Now fully awake, he saw Katya and Aiyanna standing in front of him.

"What is this? Who are you? You won't get away with this. Do you know who I am?" he yelled as he frantically yanked on the chains, trying to free himself.

"Of course I do," Katya menacingly replied.

Aiyanna giggled. "Yanking is not going to work. I tried when you left me there for what seemed like days, remember?" She walked up and blew smoke in his face while slowly moving the cigarette toward his chest.

"No, no, no…please don't," Joel shouted, panicky, while moving away as far as his bonds would let him. "Heeeelp," he yelled and yelled.

As soon as the lit cigarette touched his skin, he let out a high-pitched scream, urinated on himself, and passed out. The both of them watched in shock and disgust as the urine rolled down his inner thigh and leg. Afterward they looked at each other and burst into laughter.

"Are you fucking kidding me?!" Aiyanna responded.

While laughing hysterically, and before Aiyanna got her chance to smack the sleep out of him, Katya said jokingly, "Hold up, hold up. I got an idea."

"What are you going to do?" Aiyanna asked. Before she finished her question, Katya kicked him firmly in his testicles as if she were playing a game of kickball.

His eyes opened and his body tensed up as his face became red with pain and a thick vein started protruding out of his neck. He cried out in agony as they stood laughing at his abrupt wake-up call.

"Wakey, Wakey, eggs and bakey," Aiyanna joked.

"That looked like it hurt," Katya added as he tried to catch his breath.

"Who are you?" Joel asked while coughing from a hard testicular impact.

"Retribution is my name," Katya replied.

Hearing that, he immediately started begging, "Please, forgive me."

She moved in closer, only inches from his face, and said, "For what?"

"Everything," Joel replied.

"What specifically, would you like me to forgive you for? Because you've done a lot," Katya added.

Even though he claimed his actions to be a part of God's will, now that the punishment for those actions was laid out in front of him, Joel was too ashamed to say the words aloud. "I'm sorry," he mumbled.

"You're not sorry," Aiyanna blurted. "You said you were doing God's will, but it aroused you to see the pain you caused."

Katya joined in: "When I first met you. I thought you were my salvation, my savior who was going to save me from hell, but you are the complete opposite."

While gently caressing his silky gray-and-black hair, she said, "I hope you have a strong heart."

All of a sudden she clutched a handful and said, "Open your mouth."

"Please, no," Joel replied frighteningly

"Open your fucking mouth," she responded aggressively.

As he reluctantly opened, she quickly shoved the same club she had used to knock him out down his throat, breaking a few teeth as it entered. The club was still covered with bits of blood and fecal matter from the women he used it on.

Gently moving said club in and out of his mouth, she whispered, "Open that mouth a little wider." She moaned in pleasure as he gagged, and she added, "Just like that, and you better not throw up."

As that was happening, out of the corner of his eye he saw Aiyanna slowly making her way behind him, concealing something in her hand. She lightly grabbed his throat while Katya continued. After pleasingly licking his ear lobe, she whispered "Scream for me" before shoving a baton-like object no more than an inch in diameter, with a small spike along its body, right up his backside.

Both orifices were currently filled to the max. The moment he cried out in pain, Katya shoved the club deeper in his throat. No math could measure the powerlessness he felt. Only his previous victims could relate, and the more he struggled, the more aggressive they became.

Tears, along with snot, spit, and blood, flowed down his face, chest, and legs, but once some of it came into contact with Aiyanna's hand, it put a momentary stop to their much-needed fun.

"Eww," She disgustedly responded. "I got some of it on my hand."

Katya chuckled and replied, "Wash it off."

She then glared at Joel and added, "Now, you're going to have to pay for that."

She reached out and grabbed a scalpel from his own little setup of torture tools while pinching and pulling on his nipple. He begged "No more, please" while struggling in a futile attempt to free himself. As if his victims hadn't tried the same thing on numerous occasions.

"Stop moving, or I will cut your penis off!" Katya replied sternly.

As she moved the scalpel closer to his chest, his entire body started shaking from sheer anticipation. She glared into his eyes with a sinister smile while playfully tapping him with the sharp end of the blade. Without notice, she quickly cut off his nipple and held it in front of his face.

He screamed again while flailing around in his bonds. "Please, let me go," he cried out.

She cut off his remaining nipple, threw it in his face, and said, "She has thought of nothing else but you for years. Why would I ever let you go?"

After a moment, the realization of his situation washed over him. Now knowing he was not leaving intact, he said, "Please just kill me and get it over with."

Suddenly a brutal strike from a surgical hammer shattered his kneecap. Seconds later, another strike to the opposite knee caused his body to go limp and hang helplessly from the chains attached to the ceiling.

As he cried in pain, Katya pondered, "What can we do next?"

"Please," he kept repeating.

She grabbed his throat again, peered into his eyes as if she were looking into his soul, and said, "You remember when I kept begging you for mercy? You said to me, 'Why do you keep asking, knowing it won't help?'"

She added, "So I say to you, why do you keep asking, knowing it won't help?"

Aiyanna added, while looking over a pair of suture scissors, "You raped me until you cracked my pelvis. When I was bleeding or unconscious, it didn't matter to you. Maybe you should lose your tools for raping."

Afterward, he started praying. They both laughed as Katya responded by saying, "Funny you think prayer works."

"Please," he sobbed with a bloody rectum, broken teeth, and shattered knees.

"You're making me feel bad," Aiyanna replied as he looked upon her with those big brown puppy-dog eyes.

"I don't," Katya replied before knocking him out.

***

A while later he awoke alone, unbound, on a cold steel table with his chest wrapped in bandages, properly hooked up to an IV and blood bag. It looked as though they had cared for his wounds before departing. He took a deep breath of relief, thinking all was over and done. He was grateful for their mercy and forgiveness. However, he still couldn't walk, since both of his knees were broken, but a weird stinging sensation forced him to look over his beaten body.

"Noooooo," he shouted.

To his surprise, his genitals were missing. Only charred skin from a cauterized wound remained. He panicked and fell from the table, where he saw his missing privates on a silver platter underneath the gurney. He quickly grabbed them, and with his detached appendages in hand, he frantically crawled toward the door. Unexpectedly, a cracking sound paired with an intense pain across his back put a stop to his movement. He looked back and saw both Katya and Aiyanna standing in the corner smirking joyfully. He knew his fate was sealed. So once again he started praying: "Jesus forgive me for all my sins and save me from my turmoil."

Katya listened, took a few steps back, and said "I prayed…" as she whipped him across the chest and abdomen. "I prayed every day." And she struck him once more. "What makes you more savable than us, huh?"

"Answer me!!" she yelled.

"Forgive me, please…I'm begging you," he pleaded.

"You cut out a child's tongue, and you think you deserve forgiveness. You so-called men of God use forgiveness as a notion to get away with or justify things that you know are wrong."

She continued, "You will suffer. You will feel the pain of every woman you've ever hurt."

Not wanting to go through any more torture, he quickly reached out, grabbed a piece of broken glass, and put it to his throat in an attempt to take his own life.

Before he could do it, Katya struck him across the face with her thorned whip, detaching and eye from its socket.

"You will die on my terms," Katya responded as he lay on the floor in the fetal position.

Moments later, she continued her barrage of separating flesh from bone while yelling angrily, "Here is your forgiveness."

She didn't stop yelling or swinging her whip until he lay flat and was unreactive to the pain, which signaled his immediate death. Afterward she looked over his maimed body, which was riddled with lacerations, in pure delight, proud of herself.

"You good?" Aiyanna asked with concern. "You had a creepy, weird, happyish smile on your face."

"Yeah, I'm more than good. I'm superb," Katya joyfully replied. "Let's get back to the ship."

"Ship?" Aiyanna asked. "Like a boat?"

Katya replied, "No, a spaceship."

"You're shitting me," Aiyanna exclaimed with skepticism.

Katya chuckled. "You will see."

"Oh, and before we get there, I have to say—watch what you say to Oriyah," Katya added. "She's the tall one who looks like she could kill you with one punch."

"I think I remember her stepping through… whatever that was," Aiyanna added, "but why?"

"I don't think she likes Earth women too much," Katya replied.

"Earth women!" Aiyanna exclaimed. "They're aliens?"

"Yeah, but they look like normal women," Katya answered.

"But why does she have something against us? She is not even from this planet," Aiyanna asked.

Katya replied, "I don't know. I think it has something to do with her mother, Mayri."

"Mayri…sounds a lot like Mary," said Aiyanna. "Next, you're going to be telling me her mother was Mary Magdalene," she joked.

Katya paused, as if she had had an epiphany.

"What's wrong?" Aiyanna asked.

Before she got a chance to reply, they heard a muffled cough. Looking back, they saw Joel move his arm. "You definitely have a strong heart. I thought you were dead," Katya happily exclaimed as she walked toward him with sinister intent.

"Wait, let me finish him," Aiyanna added.

Disappointed, Katya replied, "Okay."

She then looked over his tools of torture, figuring out which she would use to end his life. "Fuck it," she said and walked over to his bloody body and stomped on the back of his head repeatedly until his body went limp.

"Just to be sure," Katya added before yanking a cross from the wall and jamming it into his heart.

"Now, let's go," she added.

Afterward the portal opened, and Katya gently grasped Aiyanna's hand and led her through.

Before anyone had a chance to react to anything, Katya asked Oriyah, "Was your mother Mary Magdalene?" Stunned, they all looked at Oriyah, anticipating her reply.

After a brief pause that seemed like forever, she replied, "Yes, but it's Mayri, not Mary."

"The prostitute or the virgin?" Natalie blurted.

A millisecond later—if you blinked, you were sure to miss it—Oriyah was inches away from her face and said, "My mother would never lie with a man, and she definitely would never sell her body for momentary gain like the women of this time."

"Jesus, I'm sorry," Natalie replied. Suddenly she was off her feet, in the air, with Oriyah's hand on her throat.

"Never mention that name in my presence. You worship a sadist…an agent of chaos. No different from the man they just ended."

"Oriyah!" Imajin shouted. Oriyah instantly dropped Natalie, and Natalie fell to the ground, coughing while rubbing her throat.

Oriyah looked at Natalie on the ground and said "I'm not sorry" before walking away.

"Good timing," Katya added sarcastically. "That was stupid of you. It's obvious you weren't listening earlier when she was venting."

"Hold up, hold up, hold up…" Aiyanna interrupted. "How is that even possible? That happened thousands of years ago."

"The women of our world age, but very, very slowly," Imajin replied.

"So how old are you and Oriyah?" Aiyanna asked.

"I honestly don't know my precise age, but Oriyah just turned two thousand," Imajin answered.

"What?!" Aiyanna exclaimed. "I'm so confused. How can someone live for that long, and how do you not know your age?"

Imajin explained, "I was not born on Oriyah's world. I was rescued from a different planet by her mother and other matriarchs who travel the universes liberating females from male kind. You age more quickly due to your habitat. The males drain your essence and your spirit. Plus, you've willingly given your souls away to men. To put it more simply, men age you."

Flabbergasted, Aiyanna sat down. "I have one more question. If her mother is in fact Mary Magdalene, was Je..."

Everyone paused and looked around, searching for Oriyah, and Amoura added, "Don't say his name."

Aiyanna continued, "Was he...her father? Or brother?"

Imajin laughed loudly. "No! They're not related, and men are not needed to procreate. We're still trying to figure out why you do need them."

Natalie interrupted, "But why does she not want to hear his name, and why does she hate us so much?"

"She doesn't hate you," Imajin replied. She sighed. "To make a long story short, he and his followers captured Mayri, and he is the one who captured, tortured, and crucified her mother for telling him no! And the women of that time watched and cheered as it happened."

After a long, silent pause, Katya replied, "No wonder she's so pissed off."

"I would be angry too," Lucia added, and they all agreed.

Except Aiyanna. "How do we know it's true?"

"We have absolutely no reason to lie to you. Believe what you want. We already know it will be next to impossible to make you believe it," Imajin answered.

"Enough of all that—I believe you," Ying interrupted. "Now, can we please stop talking and start training? So we can get to work?"

"Women are raped or murdered every second. So the longer we wait, the more we lose," Lucia added.

They all agreed.

Then Imajin turned to Amoura. "Could you take her to join the others in the healing waters?"

"Sure can," Amoura replied.

Still shocked, Aiyanna was silent. She slowly followed Amoura, shuffling her feet as she walked, contemplating the information she'd just received. It was eye opening but at the same time disheartening, the fact that her religion was based on a lie.

Afterward, Katya asked anxiously, "Where do we start?"

"The holographic training simulator. To hone your combat skills without your biosuits," Oriyah answered while mysteriously standing in the hallway. "Then we work on the mind and spirit in order to enhance your connection with the elemental mother."

Suddenly, one of the twins tugged on Oriyah's cloak and asked, "Will you teach us too?"

"Of course. But first we need you to make the other child feel right at home here. Can you do that for us?" Oriyah replied as the twins smiled with joy.

"Yes, we can," they answered.

"And where will we settle?" Farrah asked.

"Ulloa has more unbiased knowledge of this world," Oriyah replied. She then said, "Ulloa, can you find us a suitable location and construct whatever we might need to house the women we liberate, please?"

"Yes, I've already begun," Ulloa replied.

CHAPTER 14
MIND AND SOUL

"Recognize what you are:
DAUGHTERS OF THE
CELESTIAL MOTHER"

While in the training simulator, Oriyah began teaching them what she and others like her believed it meant to be female.

At the same time, Ulloa, the sentient artificial intelligence computer program, was taking it upon herself to mark the location on Earth that would best serve their lengthy purpose both tactically and geographically. In the end Ulloa chose Antarctica as their base—a patch of land in the snowy mountains near the cold coastal waters in which she instructed worker drones to build four 1,500-foot-high cylinder-shaped structures, along with an obelisk in the middle built at approximately two thousand feet tall.

While doing that, she also created significant biosignatures to identify and locate literally every female on the planet. She then sent the data to the hundreds of insect-sized mini drones roaming Earth's surface.

At the same time, the women were starting to learn about who they were. But before they officially began, Oriyah stood in front of them and started by saying, "This is going to be as hard for me as it will be for you because I've never had to explain to or teach another female about what it is to be female," Oriyah stated. She then asked, "So are there any questions beforehand?"

"Yes…lots," Ying joked. "Like, where exactly do you come from, and…"

"Are you really going to kill all the men?" Natalie blurted.

"Well, I don't really care about that," Ying added.

"Why is that a problem for you?" Oriyah replied.

"I mean, not all of them are bad. I've served with some good men," Natalie replied.

"You've said that before," Oriyah stated. "And because of that and the women on this planet who seemingly can't live without male kind, for you, I won't eradicate all of them, but their way of life is about to end, and there's no stopping us."

"They deserve it," Katya joined in.

"A tale as old as time," Natalie mumbled.

"What's that?" Katya asked confusedly.

"Women going through hell and becoming evil, vengeful against men," Natalie replied.

"Mhm," Katya added, "have you ever been raped?"

"No, but there are ways to go about this. Laws and procedures that need to be followed. We can't just go around killing every man on Earth," Natalie explained.

"Why not?" Katya asked.

"So if a woman is raped and tortured, she should just take it and accept it?" Lucia asked, agreeing with Katya.

"In a way. You should let the justice system work. That's why it's been put into place," Natalie replied confidently.

Suddenly Farrah added, "You're a military woman. I figured you would know better than to be so gullible."

"But isn't it a little cliché?" Natalie added.

"What? Killing men?" Ying replied.

"Not only that, but it's how you go about killing them! You're doing the same thing they've done to you," Natalie said.

"No shit!" Ying responded. "The others we kill will die gruesomely, but it will be relatively quick."

Katya joined in: "But those who have left their marks on the women we used to be deserved every bit of pain they experienced."

"Exactly," Elizabeth added. "You have no idea what women like us have been through, but you read about it or see it in the news and feel sad for a moment. So I guess you know, huh?"

"I'm not saying that!" Natalie exclaimed. "But you do know there are women who do really bad sexual things to children and young teenage boys, right?! And men do the things we don't want to do, like building, creating infrastructure, and re-moving garbage. Some of them actually provide a service."

At that moment the entire room fell silent as they contemplated the truth of her statement.

Suddenly, Ulloa joined in: "I'm building our base right now, and male kind is not needed. Yes, some of what you say is true. The thing about that is that in most parts of the world, men have no fear of the consequences of raping or killing. It seems to be a fantasy for most if not all of them, and af-terward they go on to live a normal life. The chaos created in your world has become normal to you. You ignore it hoping it doesn't affect you."

She then added, "The light each female holds is comparable to that of a star. Your light is like the sun behind the clouds, trying to shine through, but only slight rays of light can pierce the denseness of the clouds, and you've become accustomed to those clouds. You can see the light, but you can't fully embrace it."

She then continued while projecting a holographic image of their planet and the entire solar system in the center of the room: "In our sector of the universe, never has a female harmed another. We have no crime, no prejudice, no poverty. We don't judge one another based on beauty, brains, or material things, but then again there are no men.

"Male kind is chaos personified. Spend too much time with men, and their chaotic energy engulfs your own, and you become as they are. As it's been explained, male kind was created as the living embodiment of the void, the waste in between the stars, a virus that affects a weakened immune system. Like the common cold—it's something you've become accustomed to, but sometimes the common cold can kill because it's not something the body should be used to. The females who have diabolical intentions are suffering from a virus of the mind and spirit. They are female in body, but male kind has taken over their minds and darkened their spirits."

"But wouldn't killing men while DIABOLI-CALLY focusing on their genitals be somewhat the same as what men do?" Natalie replied sarcastically, referring to the others who had murdered men and focused more on the genitals than on the kill itself.

"They've been healed, but this creation is not easy to shrug off. It digs deep and latches on to whatever it can while doing whatever it takes to control you, whether it's a twisted form of love or physical abuse. They needed to purge that chaos from their souls," Ulloa added. "Your world produces statistics of crimes committed in every country, and male kind holds the top spot in every category. They make laws to control your bodies. They go to war and destroy the world while raping or enslaving the females as spoils of war, and you have helped them succeed by regarding women as the very things male kind promotes."

"And what's that?" Natalie asked.

"Jealous, spiteful, hateful beings who are too emotional, weak, and delicate to do anything worth doing," Ulloa answered. "The word humanity is just a way to blame both genders for the chaos in the world, but the real culprit is mankind."

"They have their own brand of justice. Now we do too!" Katya exclaimed while suspiciously glaring at Natalie.

Without notice, a bright golden light filled the entire area as if the sun had risen in the room itself. To their surprise, the light was emanating from Oriyah. She held out her hand, and the energy flowed from her core down her arm until it reached the palm of her hand and ended in something like a miniature sun hovering just centimeters above her palm.

The shocking display of energy-related abilities ceased their thoughts as they stared hypnotically at the ball of light.

Following that, Oriyah said, with the confidence of a female who is self-aware, "I'm the light that fills the void. I live amid death. I'm the natural flow that disrupts chaos, one of the many daughters of the celestial mother. She is me, I am her, and I am you. We are female."

"Wow," Amoura responded in shock. "I wish I could do that."

"You can—it's in all of us. Once you connect with the celestial mother, your natural abilities will be unlocked," Oriyah replied.

"Natural abilities? Like what?" Ying asked.

"An ability unique to your personality and passion," Oriyah answered.

"The celestial mother? Is that who you pray to? And who is this father of chaos?" Natalie inquired.

Oriyah then explained, "The mother does not require or want prayers for worship. She would like your acknowledgment." She then added, "What you call the big bang was the celestial mother separating from the father of chaos."

She then gracefully waved her hand, and the energy dissipated into nothing as flickering specks of glittery light floated around her body and disappeared. "When she freed herself, her energy expanded endlessly throughout the universe, bringing light to even the darkest corners of the cosmos. She purposely created the female in her image and as a counter to her creation. Chaos created the male in his image not only to destroy life but also to control and harness the energy of the female to imprison the celestial mother in darkness forever."

"Is that why females like you travel the universe to hunt down males?" Natalie asked.

"We don't necessarily hunt—we defend and free the women who are imprisoned in the darkness of their own minds," Oriyah passionately replied.

"But why here? Why on Earth? It's not that bad," Natalie added. "Things will change eventually."

"That bad?!?" Lucia said, slightly annoyed by her words.

"What makes you think women who are currently in the same position we were have the time to wait on 'eventually'?" Katya chimed in. "You have no idea what it's like to be drugged, beaten, and raped multiple times a day."

Ulloa abruptly interrupted their debate by unexpectedly raising a 3D hologram of Earth in the middle of the room. At the same time, numerous red and white dots appeared in rapid succession. She then stated, "Every white dot is a female content living her life, and every red dot is a female currently in some amount of turmoil, and as you can see, there are more of you that are in turmoil than there are women who are content."

"In other words, you're cool with it! You like the wool over your eyes. It blocks out the bad. Out of sight, out of mind—not your problem," Katya added with a bit of anger in her voice as she remembered that her cries for help had fallen on deaf ears, the result being that she had tricked the women she loved into slavery. The pain and regret weighed heavily on her heart.

Oriyah suddenly interrupted: "To be completely honest, my coming here was personal. I was looking for someone, but now that I'm here and I've seen your history, which is relevant to the future of this world, I know that I have to help. However, I will not force any woman to do anything against her will. It has to be her choice."

She then added, "To answer your question from earlier, I haven't interacted with any other females other than you. So I don't know for sure why the women here do the things they do, but that's something we can all find out together. My purpose is to make sure you and the planet itself are safe."

"The planet?" Natalie asked.

"Male kind are poisoning the planet, and at the same time they're poisoning you," Oriyah replied. "I understand some of you are okay with your lives, but as far as the ones who are not, I will make sure they are able to live and roam safely in their own parts of the world. In their own countries, with their own laws, militaries, technologies, and governments."

"That's reasonable, but you can't just take land!" Natalie exclaimed. "There's a right way to do it."

Ying laughed loudly and said, "We can do whatever we want."

Farrah joined in: "I'm not asking or protesting for basic human rights. We're going to take what we deserve."

"The so-called right way is their way of making us beg," Katya added.

"And I'm nobody's pet. I'm not a dog or a cat...I'm female," Lucia replied proudly.

"Why are we still having this discussion?" Elizabeth exclaimed. "We are wasting valuable time."

Oriyah then added, "Actually we're not. This room distorts time. It is neither present nor future."

"Umm, okay, I have questions, but I'm ready to train," Elizabeth replied jokingly as the others agreed. However, Natalie was slightly reluctant and unconvinced, but she figured she'd join in anyway.

"Are you ready?!?" Oriyah shouted.

"Yes!" They shouted back passionately.

Out of nowhere, five average-sized men appeared in hologram form and without warning started pummeling each of them until Oriyah canceled the simulation.

Oriyah chuckled and said, "I thought you were ready. What happened?"

"Not funny," Ying painfully groaned as they got up from the floor.

"That actually hurt," said Natalie.

"Yea, I thought it was just a hologram," Lucia joined in.

"It is, but it has mass. What is the use of training if it doesn't hurt a little bit?" Oriyah added. "Fear is a concept for the untested."

"A little warning next time," Amoura replied.

"Okay," said Oriyah. After a few moments of silence, she added with a smile, "Again."

No hesitation—this time they were ready. While implementing their fists, elbows, knees, and feet, they used precision strikes to pressure points and joints in rapid succession, devastating combinations that successfully broke down their opponents.

"That's how you do it! Don't go blow for blow—make it so fast they don't know what happened. You have faster agility with the intelligence to match. Use their aggressiveness against them," Oriyah responded excitedly. "One more time."

After a few repeated attempts that ended in the same way, Oriyah kicked it up a notch. Following that, five huge men with the aggression of rabid animals appeared in front of the women. Following that, without an ounce of logical thought, the men dashed toward them and started mercilessly beating them to no end. Blow after blow the beating continued. In the midst of their pummeling, Ying, Lucia, Katya, Amoura, Farrah, and Elizabeth all came to realize their true selves.

Oriyah patiently watched as small specks of light surrounded them. The yells of strength that preceded the light within each woman exploded simultaneously as the women violently pushed the simulated men backward into the wall. Even Oriyah felt the waves of exerted energy they released. Their energy also helped out Natalie, who seemed to be having trouble seeing her own light.

"Fēmálè," they yelled passionately together.

Oriyah smiled at their revelation of their inner light. A few moments later she repeated, "Fēmálè. See how easy it is when you know the truth?"

Natalie stood there shaken at the sight of their newfound abilities, things she herself was not able to do. She was the only one that had not broken through the layer of darkness that surrounded her spirit.

"Why me?!" she said as she closed her eyes in anger and disappointment while thinking to herself as the light from each of the women illuminated the room, piercing closed eyelids and blinding the pupils beneath.

At that moment she felt a hand on her shoulder. After opening her eyes, she saw Ying standing by her as the others looked joyfully at her. "It'll come, my sister."

Oriyah nodded in approval and said, "Again."
***

As they trained for a few days in the holographic training simulator, Ulloa finally made it past Earth's own form of artificial intelligence and was able to access all hidden government information, along with every electronic device on Earth. Every cell phone, tablet, computer, and camera was at the mercy of Ulloa.

While doing so, she came across live footage of a conference room with a still image of Oriyah projected on the wall behind a podium. She cross-referenced the faces to the data collected. In doing so, she found out that these men were the silent controllers who basically ran the world. This was a secret meeting place for the elite deep beneath the Vatican in Rome. It seemed Oriyah's appearance had ruffled a few feathers. More than enough to bring what lurked in the dark to appear in the light. So she listened as the men began to speak on the matter.

CHAPTER 15
HIS-STORY

"Ego: the confessions of man"

A Vatican priest representative by the name of Francis stood behind a podium, noticeably shaken as he cleaned his glasses with his cassock. Suddenly one of the ten or so men within the sitting audience blurted, "Why are we here? What is going on?" As the others yelled in agreement.

"Gentlemen, calm yourselves," Francis replied. He added, "Like you, I was summoned here as well."

"By whom?" another man named Charles asked.

"Whom do you think? Our benefactors…" Francis sternly replied. The room instantly fell silent; only the quiet hum of an overheated PC could be heard.

He continued, "What I'm about to share with you I've just recently learned myself, but first…we shall discuss the images projected behind me." He put on his glasses as he glared upon the screen behind him. "Judgment day may in fact be upon us."

Abdullah scoffed. "And why would you think that?"

"Because of this," Francis replied as he played the video of Oriyah's encounter with the US military. A couple of minutes later, the video stopped, and the men in attendance were shocked speechless.

"Who is she? What is she?" Abdullah asked with concern.

"That doesn't matter. What does matter is that we are being told to pool all our resources to find her. Every camera, cell phone, laptop, and satellite we have at our disposal, along with all the eyes we control."

"Why can't they…our benefactors find her?" Xian Cho asked.

Francis replied, "Because they cannot yet get involved. So here we are…"

"Why is she so important? And why can't they get involved?" Abdullah asked.

"If you want the world to remain as it is…you will find her," Francis replied.

"But you won't tell us why, but you will show us a video. That could be fake," Vladimir, a Russian politician, replied.

"You won't believe me. You won't believe what I've learned," Francis replied.

"We already know a lot," Abdullah replied. "Try us."

"If you say so," Francis said with a smirk. He then explained, "During the great war, male extraterrestrials took the original human male DNA and infused it with their own plus female DNA, and we...are the result. That is where we get our intellect. He then added, "With the strength of grizzly bears, the first men were completely barbaric and devoid of intelligence or any kind of civilized thought. They were good for fighting but not for problem-solving."

Abdullah scoffed and said, "That is nonsense."

"'The great war'?" Charles asked. "Which great war are you talking about?"

"The war of genders, you can call it," Francis replied.

"I'm guessing we won," Charles said jokingly.

Francis chuckled and added, "Apparently, but from what I hear, the first women were nothing like the modern-day females. Their knowledge of astronomy, energy manipulation, advanced weaponry, and tactics was so much of a problem that it took a variety of species of males to break through their city defenses and even more to defeat them, and history is written by the victors."

"What are you talking about now?" Abdullah exclaimed.

"Our entire history has been fabricated, intertwined with lies and a sliver of the truth," Francis replied. "We are nothing but an ongoing experiment, agents of chaos whose sole purpose is to create chaos and control the natural flow. And that flow is woman. The universe is like the nervous system, and the female is a part of that system. The perfect life form."

"And what of man?" Ivan asked.

"Chaotic negative energy," Francis replied.

"Preposterous!" Abdullah shouted while laughing condescendingly.

Irritated, Francis sighed and said, "You don't think I had the same reaction when this information was revealed to me? We might as well be demons." He pointed at the screen and added, "And she just might be a revelation."

All the men in attendance started murmuring among themselves, clearly in disagreement with what they were hearing. Their egos were wrapped around the thought of man being the superior being. He was God, the king, the messenger, the warrior and protector. Seeing themselves as nothing more than a form of chaos was clashing with the entitlement of their own beliefs.

Suddenly they all stopped abruptly. The chatter ceased when gruesome images of mangled, violated men repeated on the screen, each image being more horrible than the last.

"Jesus, what is this?" Jacob asked disgustedly.

"It seems Mary's daughter has her own disciples," Francis sarcastically replied. "If they wanted to, they could turn this world to dust, but they won't because of the other women and female animals that inhabit the planet. And believe me when I say they don't care for your young sons either."

"They did all that?" Xian Cho asked.

"Yep, and they made sure that we knew," Francis replied. He then flipped through a couple of images. He stopped and added, "By writing in blood the words 'No More' on the walls or carving them into the flesh of their victims."

"Why are they here?" Abdullah asked.

Without hesitation Francis replied, "In short, to kill all of us."

After a few seconds of silent thought, Jacob stated, "You said something about Mary's daughter?"

"Yes, that Mary," Francis replied.

"Wait! She's real?" Jacob exclaimed. "So Jesus?!"

"Real, but he's supposedly not what he has been portrayed as," Francis replied.

"Muhammad?" Abdullah blurted.

"Real, but again he is not what he has been portrayed as," Francis repeated. He then added, "Our benefactors don't believe we are strong enough to know everything, but what I do know is Mary was captured, beaten, and crucified while pregnant by Jesus and his disciples," Francis replied. "And her sisters hunted and killed them all."

"You're a priest, and you're telling me you believe this? What about your faith?" Charles asked.

Francis sighed and added, "Christianity, Islam, Judaism, Hinduism, and Buddhism—hell, even hieroglyphs—were altered or fabricated to fit the patriarch narrative while trying to erase the past. None of it really matters now because if we do not find their location, our way of life will end."

"I can't believe this," Abdullah mumbled.

"Can you believe that Atlantis wasn't a myth?" Francis replied.

"What?!" Abdullah exclaimed.

"Once called 'the Golden City' or 'the Island of the Egg,' it was built in harmony with the earth. The buildings themselves, which were a compilation of pyramids, obelisks, and other cylinder structures, were made from a combination of white stone and gold. Their structures could harness enough natural energy from the planet to power an entire country," Francis replied. He then added, "Just like Sumbala and Sumer, Atlantis was attacked by man with the help of other male beings from other worlds. We outnumbered them greatly. For every one male that fell, there were ten more to take his place." He added, "They sank Atlantis just to keep their knowledge away from us."

"This is all very confusing," Xian Cho chimed in. "And very hard to believe."

"I knew going in that this would be hard for you to comprehend," Francis added. "But we have to find these women before they reveal themselves to the world and other women try to follow suit."

"Why should it matter what they want to do?" Abdullah replied, confident in their hold on society.

"Because we cannot lose their minds. If that happens, we are finished." He then replayed the video and angrily yelled, "Look at this! This woman was able to conjure energy from nothing and use it to disintegrate three helicopters before deflecting bullets and missiles with some sort of invisible force field." As the video played, he continued, "She took a direct bullet to the fucking chest and didn't even flinch. It's almost as if she purposely let the bullet hit her to see what it felt like. He chuckled fearfully. "And she seemed to use some sort of telekinesis to lift them out of the water and crush them slowly like they were nothing but pieces of paper. She broke almost every bone in their bodies before dropping them back into the ocean, and she did all that while walking on the surface of the water!"

Francis then added, "With their numbers now, what would happen if all of them had these kinds of powers? What would we do then? Books have been rewritten; lines have been crossed; chemicals in food, thought manipulation, and plenty more have been used to keep the human female docile and content. We can't lose that hold."

Charles joined in: "Maybe we could meet with them and discuss…"

"No," Francis interrupted. "That will not happen."

"We are billions; they are only a few. I don't see the need to worry," Abdullah stated.

Francis threw up his hands in frustration and said, "Did you not see the video or hear a damn word I've been saying?"

"What are you not telling us?" Abdullah shouted as the others agreed with his conclusion.

Francis turned to look at one of the men sitting in a dark corner of the room. He nodded before Francis started to explain: "After the great war, this planet was set to be destroyed by ancient dark entities so it could never be a haven for females ever again, but ancient aliens pleaded on Earth's behalf by making this world a source for chaos. Hence we are always in a state of conflict."

"Why are they so important?" Xian Cho asked.

"Every act of violence toward women releases a certain energy that these entities consume for mere pleasure. Since the female is directly connected to life, a tortured life or a corrupt soul not only pleases them, it gives them strength as well. The more pain she endures, the more energy is released upon death, and if she has already given her soul away to any religious male savior, it is just icing on the cake. They praise darkness without even knowing it." He then added, "She is the light. A light we need to see ourselves."

"And what do I need to see?" Abdullah asked with arrogance.

"That your Kaaba with its black stone is one of the sources that cause and collect chaotic energy in this world. Those dark entities I mentioned use it like a water fountain," Francis said with arrogance of his own. "All our lives are on the line. The aliens who created us will destroy every human on this planet and start over before they let it be taken back."

"You mean Allah?" Abdullah replied.

"There are no gods, just advanced beings playing a game," Francis replied, emotionless, as he removed the rosary cross from around his neck and added, "and I for one am happy to hear it! This information was given to me by beings who are older than the oldest fossil. Their knowledge of the universe far exceeds our own."

Abdullah groaned loudly, then slammed his hands down on the table and shouted, "This is ridiculous. You're telling me I'm an experiment, genetically enhanced with female DNA to become the man I am? On top of that, you're telling me my belief is a complete fabrication, a game to aliens, and a woman is superior to me? A woman may have birthed me, but my father made me. Without him none of us would ever be. Man or woman!"

"Not true—without man woman will revert to her authenticity. In other words, we are their demons," Francis replied.

"No!" Abdullah exclaimed. "You may have lost your faith, but I will never dishonor the father. No woman is superior to me. I'm not Iblis; I am a child of Allah."

"If your god is an alien, then, yes, you're right," Francis replied.

"No, I will not believe that. I will not…" Abdullah continued shouting. "What if we say no? Let our so-called benefactors find them."

Moments later, the entire room felt an uneasy, unearthly presence. Then the lone man sitting in the dark corner stood up and slowly walked toward Abdullah and said, "The inevitable happens…sooner rather than later." His eyes then suddenly turned snakelike and became bright with a yellowish glow.

As Abdullah sat there hypnotized, the unknown man gradually morphed into a reptilian alien right before their eyes, revealing his true nature. The alien's tongue flicked in and out while it moved its head side to side. It then said in a low, guttural, demonic tone, "Pray to me."

"I'm sorry. Forgive me," Abdullah replied as he shook from complete fear.

"We don't know the word," the reptilian being replied.

Then, out of nowhere, it opened its mouth as black acidic drool rolled down the corners of its mouth and melted through the dense marble floor as if it were as hot as magma. Its jaw unhinged like that of an anaconda preparing for a big meal.

"Please," Abdullah begged.

The creature then slowly closed its mouth as Abdullah sat there momentarily relieved, while the others looked on, terrified by the sudden revelation. It then sniffed the air, seemingly pleased with their fear, and without warning it bit off Abdullah's head and swallowed it whole, slurping up his spinal cord as if it were a spaghetti noodle. As blood spouted from the remaining part of his neck and shoulders, the reptilian creature drank from his headless body just as if it were a water fountain, giving sight to Francis's words about chaos.

However, Francis himself showed no fear. He said, as their benefactor washed down his food with a bloody, nutritious drink, "There is so much more to tell you, but we simply don't have the time. If we don't find them…"

A loud growl resonated throughout the room before the creature added, "The inevitable."

CHAPTER 16
THE INEVITABLE

"Change"

After lifting the veil that the chaotic males had pulled down over their faces, they emerged from the training simulator with a newfound purpose. Their connection with one another, along with the knowledge from Oriyah's lessons, lit a fire in their soul. The ways of male kind on planet Earth would soon come to a painful, abrupt end, and it went without saying that the satisfaction would be a tremendous bonus. Now they were more aware of self, nourished by the light, with a sensible mission of freedom and safety for all women. The female was all that mattered because she had endured more than enough: a society that revolved around the patriarchy. The inevitable uprising was well at hand.

However, before any of that could transpire, they were called to the cargo hold as Ulloa took them to see their new home. When they approached, the cargo door gradually opened, letting in the cold Arctic wind. As the bright sun bounced off the pure white snow, the glare itself temporarily blinded the crew, but as their vision cleared, they saw four tall towers surrounding a center obelisk. The outsides of the towers were like mirrors reflecting the sky, the clouds, the sunlight, and all their surroundings. The center obelisk stood with even more beauty, as it was solid gold.

"Beautiful, and huge," Ying replied as they all agreed. "Where are we?"

"Antarctica. Schematics of each structure will be downloaded onto your MUGs momentarily," Ulloa replied. "Each building harnesses the wireless energy of the world power grid. Each one was built specifically to coincide with certain constellations."

"Amazing," Natalie added. "I'm not complaining, but it's a little barren with all the snow."

"And cold," Farrah added. "Couldn't we find an island to live on?"

"Some fun in the sun with beaches and margaritas and stuff! Now that would've been nice," Ying joked.

"I don't know what a margarita is, but I can do something about the other stuff," Oriyah replied.

"Oh, when this is all over we are definitely going to show you," Ying replied.

Oriyah smiled and kissed Imajin on her lips and said to the group "Watch with more than your eyes" before casually falling backward out of the hatch, which was still hovering a thousand feet in the air. Shocked, they all watched and waited in anticipation.

With the enhanced senses that were achieved during their training, they watched with the vision of eagles as she approached the ground. Expecting a hard impact, they were surprised to see nothing happened to the ground below. Not a flake of the pristine snow was moved from beneath her feet. It was as if she literally landed on air. Afterward, she stood there for a moment and knelt down. She dug her bare hands deep into the slushy snow and closed her eyes.

Moments later, a golden light started to gather around her as the nanites that made up her biosuit suddenly started to vibrate. The luminance of the light grew brighter and bright until it seemingly reverted back onto Oriyah and disappeared. Following that, Oriyah stood up and leapt into the air, landing back on the ship with ease.

"So no margarita?" Ying sarcastically added. "So disappointing."

"What did you do?" Natalie asked.

"You will see when we get back," Oriyah replied with a smile as the hatch closed behind her. "Where to first?"

"Afghanistan," Farrah blurted while twisting the tip of her blade back and forth on the tip of her middle finger. "Specifically Kabul."

"Kabul, Afghanistan: under Taliban rule from 1996 to 2001. The Taliban took power once again in 2021," Ulloa announced.

Farrah added, "And the women there are isolated, suffocated, and being forced to live like the entire country is a prison, but a prison only for women. The men are free as long as they adhere to the teachings of Islam. There are a lot of men that need to be eradicated. They see women as nothing but a convenient inconvenience."

"Afghanistan it is," Oriyah replied without hesitation as she sensed the experience in her heart.

"What's the plan?" Lucia asked.

"Based on the data collected—" Oriyah replied.

Before she had a chance to finish her thoughts, Farrah interrupted by saying, "I know this place, and I know their ways. Women are inside most of the time unless they're accompanied by a man." She scoffed and added, "They can't even go to school or ride a bicycle." She then continued, "So at night, only the Taliban will be outside patrolling. I propose we silently kill as many as we can under the cover of darkness and leave their bodies for the others to find the next morning."

"Talk about making some noise," Ying jokingly responded.

They all laughed as Ulloa plotted a course to the country of Afghanistan.

"Let's go murder some people," Ying said with excitement.

"No, not people…men, and invasive viruses. That sounds better to me," Lizzy replied.

They laughed once more and agreed with her conclusion.

Before they took off, Imajin stated, "Maybe the others and I should stay here while you all go. We can get a chance to explore our new home and prepare for the others you save."

"Are you sure?" Oriyah asked.

"Yes, I think they need to take some time and take all of it in," Imajin replied. "They're hopeful, but I can sense the hopelessness stalking their spirits."

"Okay," Oriyah replied. "Call me if you need or want me to do something. I will be here within the blink of your eyes."

"Of that I have no doubt, my light," Imajin added confidently. "Be careful and stay out of trouble."

They all suddenly started snickering.

"What?!" Imajin exclaimed.

Oriyah leaned in and lightly kissed Imajin on her forehead, then the tip of her nose, and on to her lips, while gently stroking the side of her face and whispering all sweet-like, "I don't think I'm going to be able to do any of that."

They all burst out with laughter. "Nope, not even a little bit," Katya joined in.

"Well, just come back to me," Imajin said while joining in on the laughter.

"Now, that I will always and forever do," Oriyah replied with another gentle kiss.

"Aww, you two are just too cute," Ying added while making a heart with her hands. After which Lucia and Katya shared a quick glance and hopeful smile.

Soon after, Imajin, along with the others, vacated the ship and were now safely inside one of the four buildings that now occupied the open area of the trans-Arctic mountains near the Ross Sea as they set off on their mission to end the mental and physical enslavement of women, although the satisfaction of removing the worst types of men would be almost orgasmic in comparison. It was safe to say that darkness would see the light fight back with the strength of truth behind it.

While hovering above Kabul, Afghanistan, way later than the imposed curfew, they scanned the city for men and women who were currently outside their homes. Knowledge of weapons and ammo, along with anatomy and physiology, was information deemed important to their mission. They were utilizing every speck of their technology and intuition to ensure the uprising of women. Their strategy and tactics would prove to be more than Sun Tzu himself could counter.

"This place is bigger than I expected. I wonder how many are on patrol," Amoura stated.

"Eighty-six soldiers on tonight's rotation, and they impose harsh laws on anyone caught after curfew," Ulloa joined in.

"Twenty," Farrah added.

"What's that?" Ying asked.

"That's how many of them I'm going to re-move from this world," Farrah replied.

"Oh, so we're keeping score," Katya joined in. "Twenty-five."

After which they all started shouting numbers: twenty-three, twenty-seven, twenty-nine…

"Eighty," Oriyah replied with a grin.

"Hold up! You're in on this?" Ying replied. "I quit."

"Right," Lucia added. "You are supposed to be like a supervisor. Just watching and making sure we don't mess up. It's not fun if you play."

"Wait, wait, wait," said Katya. "Remember she told us that we have the potential to be just like her. So let's give it a try."

Ying walked over to the much taller Oriyah and looked up at her with a serious mean mug and said, "Eighty-one…boom! Whatchu got?"

They all burst into laughter again before real-izing that the time to attack was now. No more jokes, no more games—this was that moment. While checking their gear and running diagnos-tics, Oriyah stated, "No energy blasts or blunt objects. Swords only. We do this quietly. Severe the head or open the neck so they can't alert anyone." They all nodded in agreement. She then said, "Ulloa, please give us a portal to their tallest building, and send the city's complete infrastructure to our MUGs, please, and…"

Ulloa interrupted and said, "Watch your backs."

"Yes, and do as you see fit to the perpetrators," Oriyah replied.

"With a fair amount of pleasure," Ulloa added.

"I just love her," Ying added gleefully as they stepped through the portal.

They stood atop the Kabul Tower in the dead of night, not a female in sight. There were only soldiers patrolling the city. The conditions were perfect cloudy, cold, with a slight drizzle. Before they went to work, Oriyah said to the group, "Anarchy or contentment?"

Soon after that question, the nanites that made up their biosuits started constructing dual swords in their hands as Katya replied "The answer is obvious" before leaping off the tower while simultaneously cloaking, becoming nearly invisible to the naked eye.

In the meantime Ulloa, the sentient artificial intelligence program, was taking it upon herself to shut down every porn site on the net, including all the heinous acts seen on the dark web. Not only did she wirelessly crash the servers using Earth's own satellites, she also made her own profile on every social media platform while constantly posting pictures and videos of crimes carried out against women in every country. The algorithm she created made sure they would appear to all users as they scrolled. Other than that, droves of men proven to be pedophiles and rapists suddenly died from an unknown source.

After an hour or so, and several severed heads and sliced throats later, they heard a whisper over their communicator. "Hey, collect some of the heads and bring them to me," said Farrah.

"Umm, what?" Natalie replied. "Why do you need the heads?"

"I want to scrawl out the words "NO MORE" with heads around the Abdul Rahman. So when they come to worship they will be in for a horrific surprise," Farrah replied.

For a few moments, silence ensued over the radio. "That is just so creepy and crazy, and I just love it," Ying replied. "I'm coming."

By the time they got to her, their swords looked like shish kebabs skewered through human heads. The only thing missing was the grill. "This is going to be such a mindfuck when they see this," Lucia responded.

"I know, right?" Farrah replied while nudging the heads into position with her feet. "And make sure the faces are showing. Just think about it— they're going to have to clean up the heads and see the last terrified, confused looks on their faces. The whole country, if not the world, will be scared." She giggled and added, "While close to a mosque! They will think it's the end of times."

"It is…for them," Oriyah added. "Now let's get moving. The sun will be up soon."

"I'm finished," Farrah replied as Ulloa opened the portal leading back to their ship.

Suddenly, Ying jumped as high as she could in the air and landed. She smiled and said, "Now that is a work of art. I just had to see it from above."

"Why didn't you just wait until we were back on the ship?" Amoura asked.

"Because I didn't think of that," Ying embarrassedly replied. They all giggled and walked through the portal back to the ship.

"Where to next?" Farrah excitedly asked.

"Boko Haram," Amoura replied with a seriousness in her eyes. "Can we find their location?"

"Boko Haram? Aren't they the ones who abducted a bunch of girls from a school?" Natalie asked.

"Yes, 276, of which only 50 or so managed to escape by jumping off their captors' trucks. The others were forced to be suicide bombers or sex slaves," Amoura replied.

"Ulloa's already on it," Oriyah added.

"She's found them already?" Amoura exclaimed.

"Yeah, well, one of their compounds in the jungles of Congo, Africa," Oriyah replied. "You all should really get used to your MUGs. All the data she has we have. They can also become energy shields and short-range energy cannons."

"Seriously?" Katya added, shocked.

Like a frustrated teacher, Oriyah groaned and shook her head. "Did any of you even bother with going through the instructions?"

"What instructions?" Lizzy asked. "When you handed them to us, you didn't give us any instructions."

Oriyah took a deep breath. "Each of you, tap the center of your MUG, please."

The screen itself opened, revealing something that resembled contact lenses and an earbud, after which Lizzy said confusedly, "Contact lenses and an earbud?"

Oriyah then explained, "That is an ocular device that gives you detailed readouts of your surroundings, and this is a device for communicating with one another and so that Ulloa can relay information to you if needed."

She then stopped abruptly and confusedly asked, "Wait! Back in Afghanistan how did you see where the males were, and how did you talk with one another?"

"I was just speaking, like, at or…like into the screen," Farrah replied.

Ying added, "And I just ran around jumping from roof to roof looking for them."

Oriyah put her head down while placing her hands over her face, trying to hold back laughter, and said, "No wonder it took you so long. Ulloa, why didn't you tell them?"

"It was humorous watching them run around," she replied.

"You watched us," Natalie exclaimed. "What if something had happened?"

"I was watching. Nothing was going to happen," Ulloa replied.

"How can you be so sure?" Natalie asked.

Suddenly a small insect-sized drone appeared, hovering near each of them. "When you're out, they are always with you," Ulloa added.

"Please don't spread yourselves out too much," Oriyah replied with concern.

"Isn't she a program? That's pretty much her job, right?" Natalie added.

Oriyah turned to her and said, "Again! She is not a program. She is conscious and alive."

"Well, I blame Oriyah," Ying teasingly blurted, changing the subject. "You're supposed to be like our supervisor or teacher and let us know, but you didn't, so you get the blame, not Ulloa."

"What?! I thought you knew because you didn't ask," Oriyah replied.

"Well, we didn't, but now we do. But we still can blame you," Lucia added.

Before she had a chance to reply, Ulloa interrupted. "We're here."

***

As they hovered above a patch of cleared-out jungle in the Congo. A small compound with a few structures and handmade huts was occupied with multiple intoxicated Boko Haram rebels armed with automatic weapons and the aggression to use them.

Upon first glance only five women were visible, and each of them was in bad condition. Meanwhile, some of the men were walking in and out of an entrance dug into the hillside.

"Ulloa, can you get a drone in there and see what's going on?" Oriyah asked.

"Of course," Ulloa replied.

Seconds later, they all flinched and jumped back, flailing around like they were shadowboxing. "Whoa! What's that?" Ying yelled.

Oriyah giggled. "She connected you to the drone so you can see what it sees through the ocular device."

"Just call it a contact lens," Elizabeth replied.

"Well, she connected your contact lens to the drone. You can also hear what it hears," Oriyah replied.

"Okay, pretty cool," Ying added. "Would've been nice when we were in…" But before she could finish her statement, they started to see what was hidden in the hillside. The entrance led to a cave system that housed a dozen women chained and caged in deplorable conditions. Covered in rags, they lay in their own feces as rat- and mouse-sized cockroaches crawled over their bodies. It seemed they were just waiting for death.

As the drone carried on analyzing the cave system, they came upon another opening where women were being cleaned and prepared to be sold to whoever had a few dollars. While some were being sanitized, others were being brutally gang-raped by the rebels. Some were boys as young as ten participating in the disgusting act.

An angry and anxious Oriyah said, "Let's go!"

"No, wait," Amoura responded.

"What? Why!?" Oriyah shouted.

"Watch," Amoura replied.

"Why would I want to watch?" Oriyah said angrily.

"They will be healed, correct?" Amoura asked.

"Yes," Oriyah quickly replied.

"So please watch and look at their eyes," Amoura added.

After a few moments, she asked Oriyah, "What do you see?"

Staring intently into their eyes while trying to look past the disgusting act in order to understand her point, Oriyah replied, "Nothing. No tears, no anger, no emotion at all."

"Numb—that's how most of us are now, and that's how we were when you met us. We put all our emotions in a box and kept them there. We were tired of fighting and losing. Then we just became content with what was," Amoura replied. "I just wanted you to understand us as a whole."

"You can't combat callousness with compassion," Oriyah replied, "but I do understand and will do my best to be more sympathetic. Now let's go."

Before they stepped through the portal, she added, "Oh! When the fight starts…don't cover your face. Let them see we're female."

"Ha!" Amoura blurted with excitement. "I can't wait to see what they do," she said as they walked through the opening.

Moments later, while cloaked, they stood just outside the compound, near the entrance into the cave system. Oriyah whispered over the communicator, "This time I will watch. What's your plan?"

"Make them come to us," Amoura said. "Wound one—make him cry for help. Kill the rest once they get here. My mother told me stories of how they used to do it in her village. The same village where those girls were taken. We use their tactics on them."

After a brief pause of heartfelt sentiment, they all heard a bloodcurdling scream that sounded like it was coming from all directions. Following that, they saw Ying plunge her blade into the bladder of a man who was urinating and give it a little twist to inflict as much pain as possible before joyfully skipping her way back to the group.

"Um…I think that'll work," Amoura said, grimacing.

Within a matter of seconds, other Boko Haram soldiers started to converge on the screaming and bleeding man's location. More than a few meters away, the ladies waited patiently for more to show up. Before long more than twenty or so men had gathered. While some scanned their surroundings looking for the cause of their fellow rebel's mishaps, the others attended to their fallen brother.

They gradually started getting closer and closer to the nearly invisible women. Without notice, the once light drizzle turned into a heavy downpour. During that time they caught the suspicious eye of one of the rebels because the rain itself revealed their silhouettes. Noticing that they were no longer able to remain unseen, the female warriors uncloaked right before the eyes of AK-47-wielding rebels, with Amoura standing front and center.

The rebels started aggressively shouting as they waved their weapons around, trying to intimidate the women into submission, not knowing that these women submitted to no man.

Suddenly one of them tried to grab Amoura by her arm, and without hesitation she drew back and punched the man in his chest so hard that the force sent him flying backward nearly twenty feet away. Some of the rebels shared a look of concern, while some became more aggressive.

Amoura stood tall, gazing over her fist, enamored by the strength of the punch itself. "Wow, I didn't expect that." She then held out her hand, and the rebels watched as her nanites constructed a basic baseball bat right before their eyes.

"This is going to be fun," Ying added.

The confused soldiers immediately started firing their weapons, only for their bullets to be reflected by an energy shield produced by the women's MUGs. Now with empty clips and unbothered women, they took worried looks at each other and immediately started to reload. With the men's weapons reloaded and one ready in the chamber, the women suddenly started laughing hysterically at their feeble attempts to delay the inevitable.

Without warning, the man at the back of the pack suddenly started gurgling. When they looked back, he was frozen, not moving a single inch, just shaking. Following that, he dropped his weapon. Seconds later, his arms from the bicep down fell to the ground. Next, his shirt exposed a cut across his chest. Afterward, the area from his chest up gradually separated from the rest of his body and slid to the ground, divulging a still-beating half heart. A look of horror filled their souls as blood spewed from his aorta.

While still standing behind him, paused in a pose following the decapitation of said rebel, Elizabeth kicked the remaining part of the lower half of his body over and said to the rebels, "No more. You will all die here, today."

Soon after, another rebel cried out in pain. They looked and saw their fellow rebel hovering in the air with Ying's spear protruding out of his stomach. While he was still screaming from the pain, Lucia cut off his face, starting at his forehead and ending at his chin. The remaining men watched as it fell to the grass. Following that, Ying pinned him to the ground and used her foot to pull her spear from his deceased body. With the rain still pouring, they cloaked once more in order to frighten the already terrified rebels. Panicked, the rebels instantly started running and randomly firing in different directions.

The youngest of them, boys no older than thirteen, were too scared to do anything. They dropped their guns and stood in place, frozen from fear as they watched bodies being mangled and decapitated by an invisible foe. The screams and cries of agony had each of them crying hysterically while pissing themselves uncontrollably. Entrails, severed limbs, and dying rebels gasping for their last breaths, grateful that death would relieve their pain, forced them to think to themselves that they were next. That their fates were inevitable.

When every single rebel was dead and blood drenched the soil below, the women wasted no more time before freeing those who were imprisoned by the rules of war in which women were a convenient prize. A total of 36 women were saved out of the 276 that were taken. The others had been either sold into slavery, used as suicide bombers, or beaten and raped to death by the so-called freedom fighters who wanted to create a pure Islamic state ruled by sharia law. A notion no different from that of the men that killed and defiled for their Christian beliefs, and every time, it was the women and girls who suffered the most.

The number of women saved dwindled when they found four women lying on the dirt floor in a large room, women who were too close to death to be healed. Their breasts had been cut off and burned, and their genital areas looked as though they had been ripped open.

"They left them there as a warning to us. Never try and escape," one of the captured women said tearfully.

As anger and sadness filled their hearts and minds, Amoura replied with regret, "I shouldn't have made you wait. I'm sorry."

"It is not your fault," another woman added. "This is what they do."

She and the others kneeled by their bodies with tears flooding their eyes. As they drew closer and closer to life's end, Oriyah got down on both her knees and said with passion and sincerity,

"Mother, let her rest. Let her sleep. This unnatural world would not let her be. Let her live again in the arms of your light, without torment and pain-free. Don't let her spirit burn in the fire. We are you. We are Fēmálè, and I'm Oriyah." The end of her acknowledgement perfectly synced with their last breath.

Seconds later, during their moment of silence for the victims, a portal suddenly opened in the doorway, disclosing Imajin on the other side. Following that, the deceased female bodies slowly started to rise and gather together in a straight line and seemed to float in the air.

"Take care of them," Oriyah said.

"I will," Imajin replied with sentiment.

Afterward, they looked back and saw Oriyah with her arm stretched out while simultaneously moving her hands and arms as if she were gently pushing something. The deceased women then slowly started to make their way through the portal, while the others followed behind, one by one.

The portal closed, and Katya asked, "Was that telekinesis?"

"Something like that," Oriyah replied before hastily exiting the rancid cave to get some fresh air.

Outside, the young boys were still standing in a puddle of their own making.

"What about them?" said Natalie.

"What about them?" Oriyah replied emotionlessly.

"So we're just going to leave them here?" Natalie added.

"We didn't come here for them," Oriyah stated.

"We can at least help them," Natalie added.

"Okay, you're right," Oriyah replied while briskly walking toward the children. She said while bending over close to them, "If you ever harm a female, I will do you just like we did your little friends. I don't care what you do to each other, but leave women out of it. Do you understand?" The little frightened boys quickly nodded. Following those stern words, Oriyah looked at Natalie and said, "How's that for help?"

Right before heading through back to the ship, Ying yelled, "One of them is still alive."

"Well, kill him and let's go," Oriyah replied.

Ying menacingly looked over the man's bleeding body and said, "Nah, I think I'll let him live to tell the tale." She bent over toward the man and added, "Now say 'Thank you for giving me life.'"

After a few moments of silence, she plunged her spear into his thigh. He painfully cried out while saying, "Thank you for giving me life."

Ying removed her weapon. She shook her head and said, "You took too long," and with the tip of her spear she cut his neck, just enough to nick the carotid artery, and added, "I guess you can call us karma. You've hurt and killed women. Now a woman has killed you." He tried to put pressure on his neck in his fear of death—a futile attempt to stop the bleeding. "How ironic," she added with a joyful smile.

The last thing he saw as his life slipped away was the whimsical skipping of a woman who did not adhere to the patriarchy. This was something different. Was this the inevitable?

Now back on the ship and anxious to move on from this location, the women waited patiently for their next plan of action, but before that could happen, Oriyah had a word with Natalie, though her voice was aimed at all of them. She said loud and clear, "I understand…"

After hearing the tone in her voice, everyone looked her way as she continued, "You have some connection to the men in this world, a brother, an uncle or father…whatever. What I was taught is that males, whether they are children or adults, if they don't see the wrong in their ways or if wrong-doing benefits them in any way, will do what they want. No amount of mothering will ever change that. You only delay the inevitable. Out of respect for the women here, those boys aren't lifeless, but believe me when I say I don't care. I'm trying to be understanding, but I will not put our lives at risk for your unwavering compassion for chaos." She shrugged her shoulders and added calmly with a smile, "You can either get with it or go back to what you know. The choice is yours."

She then completely changed the subject; she didn't care for anyone's rebuttal. Her patience with Natalie was near its end, but knowing and understanding that the women here had been mentally and physically beaten into what seemed like eternal submission was something that couldn't be overlooked. It was not their fault that they felt a connection to man. The patriarchy needed to crumble, but they were too attached to let it happen.

She continued, "You all are very capable women, but you're not maximizing the potential of your biosuits. Remember, the nanites are synced to you and only you. They have a hive mind, and you are the mind. If you think it, they do it, and if you can't gather your thoughts, you can also program them to respond to certain words and phrases or even gestures and movements."

She added, "To a certain extent, they can take any form you choose."

"Like what? A person or object?" Amoura asked.

Unexpectedly, Oriyah's biosuit slowly started covering her head, face, and body. Afterward, the nanites started to mimic Natalie as if they were identical twins, reflecting every feature of her body. Seconds later, they mimicked one of the rebels killed during their tussle with Boko Haram.

Oriyah then stated, "We usually don't use these features of deception on other women. Because we don't deceive one another. Manipulation is a male trait that shall not be used on one another."

Afterward, her face and head transformed into different animal heads…lioness, tiger, and wolf. "While you're using the biosuit as a mask, it not only enhances your hearing and sight but will also give you visuals of what's behind you while acting on its own in order to protect you."

"What else can you do?" Katya asked.

"That was the nanites," Oriyah stated.

"Yes, I know that," Katya replied. "We know you're super strong, super fast, and super smart. We saw energy accumulate in your hand and watched you play with it like a toy and…"

"And disintegrate three helicopters without injuring the people in them. Oh! And walk on water…literally," Natalie blurted.

"Umm, wow! Didn't know all that, but… wow!" Katya replied.

"And don't forget—she playfully jumped out of the ship, and right before she hit the ground, she stopped in midair," Elizabeth added.

"Can you fly?" Ying blurted out excitedly.

Oriyah said not a word—she just tilted her head and smiled. As they stared intently at her, waiting for a reply, she said, "You will see—if you stay, and I hope you do, because there's so much more for you to see and learn. The universe is because you are."

"Aww, she's starting to grow fond of us now," Ying teasingly replied while playfully poking her in the side.

"Don't push it," Oriyah jokingly replied while turning around to see the next locations Ulloa had chosen.

"And back to being mean," Lucia quipped.

Farrah added, "She's like the grumpy older sister."

"OOOOOOlder sister," Ying joked.

"Way old!" Amoura exclaimed.

"Super old," Katya chimed in.

"Really, really old," Elizabeth teased.

"You're making it sound bad," Oriyah replied.

"Yeah, that was the purpose," Amoura said sarcastically as they had a good laugh at Oriyah's expense.

"Ha ha!" Oriyah joked. She then added, "You had your laugh; now let's get back to it." They all shouted in agreement, excited and enthused about the fights to come.

"I think I will just sit back and watch," Natalie blurted.

They all looked over at her, confused as to why.

"Your connection to them is still…connected," Oriyah replied.

"Yes," Natalie said. "I will get there, but for now, I will watch and learn."

"Understandable. Stay near me. At all times," Oriyah added.

Over the next couple of weeks, they completed dozens of missions while breaking only to eat and drink. They tore through country after country, changing the narrative that was women. Payment was due, and it was now time to collect.

They started in Iran and disguised themselves as ordinary woman without their hijabs and cut down every man that tried to enforce the biased laws, and they then made a detour to the Arab republic of Syria and rescued a hundred or so female political prisoners and Yezidi women from the clutches of man. Their work in Honduras and neighboring countries that were considered the most dangerous places to be a woman left skinned members of the cartels and other gangs at the doorsteps of fathers and sons alike as a warning. Their escapades in the rape capital of South Africa had men terrified to leave their homes because of the castrated men that were randomly found around the country, alive while lying in puddles of blood. Yemen and West Africa held the same kind of men and paid the same price for their genital mutilation of women. India, Sri Lanka, and others felt the female rage when they started finding their men beaten within an inch of their lives. In China, Japan, and the UK, "grooming gangs" were found and executed without mercy for their assaults against the youngest of girls. Multiple cities in the United States and neighboring islands held hundreds of children and women who were bought and sold in the sex trade but were now saved by these unwavering daughters of the celestial mother.

Nobody was spared, neither the weak nor the powerful, the rich nor the poor. Fortune 500 company CEOs, celebrities, regular working men, homeless men, or political giants. No man, no matter his status, was exempt from these killers of men. It was the purge of an invasive rhetoric. However, if a man had not harmed a woman, he was not harmed.

As satisfying as it was to dismember and destroy the vilest of males, there was disappointment because the number of women that actually wanted to join them wasn't as large as Oriyah had initially thought. Most wanted what was clearly understandable. Which was to go home to be with their loved ones.

Some did not join because of other matters. Some wouldn't have felt comfortable or normal in an all-female society. They accepted the healing, but not the knowledge, solely because Oriyah's was a civilization of women. A few of the others saw them as monsters for their brutality and fled without so much as a thank-you. Out of the thousands saved, only a few hundred remained.

CHAPTER 17
SAFE HAVEN

"Heaven"

Nevertheless, even after a bunch of disappointment, the warrior women were still enthused and anxious to continue. They reveled in their success by reminiscing and demonstrating past acts of male decapitation. Their teacher, on the other hand, was not feeling the joy. Despite feeling discouraged and a bit angry, Oriyah put on a fake smile for her companions. She couldn't help but wonder why their actions hadn't gotten any media attention worldwide. Is it deliberate, or do we need to do something more drastic?

Impulse whispered, "Drastic," but her mother's voice replied with "Think before you act." But that major part of her, the part that craved a challenging fight, was another voice of its own design. Her fists were itching and her body was aching to use the strength she was born with because she, for one, had never faced a strong male or used her full potential. So in conclusion…drastic measures it was.

"Ulloa," Oriyah asked. "Have you seen any of our efforts appear anywhere on the net?"

"A few, but most are taken down almost instantly. Even their obituaries are falsified. Someone is covering up our efforts."

"We need to be seen by the world. Being unknown won't produce any significant change right now, and this world itself is almost at the point of no return. So maybe we should," Oriyah replied.

Ulloa then added, "Well, they're having a diplomatic peace summit that's currently almost about to start. It's considered unprecedented because of the number of countries that have agreed to meet."

"A peace summit, huh?" Oriyah said with a mysterious grin. After a brief moment of contemplation, she said, "Take us back to home base."

"What? Why?" Amoura asked.

"I need to see Imajin before we go," Oriyah replied.

"Where are we going?" Katya asked.

"To a peace summit," Oriyah answered.

"Hmm, we're making some more noise?" Ying asked.

"Yup! A loud one," Oriyah replied.

"Finally," Katya replied loudly as the others agreed. "I mean, what we're doing is good, but we need to go bigger. The men need to see women without any fear whatsoever. They have to see what we are capable of and…"

She fell silent midsentence. All the chatter stopped as they approached their base in Antarctica. The once barren tundra was now an oasis that covered at least ten square miles, with the five buildings directly in the middle.

The snow-covered ground was now similar to a jungle, complete with a beautiful serene waterfall that fed into a freshwater lake with white sandy shores. A multitude of different species of tree life filled the oasis. Some were as tall as twenty-story buildings while being nearly ten meters in diameter. There was a staggering variety of plant life and dense vegetation that could feed a small town. Vines with colorful flowers along their stems had attached themselves to each building, making the spectacular sight even more breathtaking. Their home was purely enchanting, a paradise for all intents and purposes.

As they flew over the land, they saw little girls joyfully swimming and splashing around in the lake, while others played in the tall trees. Some of the women were relaxing lakeside in the sun, while others roamed the jungles, exploring and collecting fruits for later consumption. They all seemed very happy and comfortable in their new home.

"How?" Amoura asked in shock as she gazed at the landscape.

"Is that what you were doing when that light gathered around you after you jumped from the ship?" Katya asked.

"Yes," Oriyah replied.

"But how?" Amoura repeated.

"I just asked her. If you can hear her, she can hear you," Oriyah responded.

"I wish I could do that," Lucia replied.

"You can," Oriyah responded. "Remember, I am you and we are one. A part of the same life source."

After that, the ship landed safely on the roof of one of the buildings. As they exited the ship, a few of the women shouted, "Welcome to heaven."

"Heaven?" Oriyah said confusedly.

"It's what we call paradise," Aiyanna replied.

"And we all love it here. It's like heaven," Prisha joined in.

"Well, I'm very happy that you do," Oriyah replied. She then looked around for Imajin, but she was nowhere to be found.

"You all are settling in well," Katya said. "Where is your daughter?"

"She's playing by the lake with the twins, along with the other children, as happy and strong as can be," Prisha replied joyfully.

"How about the others we sent back?" Amoura asked.

"They were a little scared at first, but they've now healed physically and spiritually. They've settled in nicely. Plus, Ulloa helped out a lot. She's been nothing but compassionate to our needs," Aiyanna replied. "The other women know who you are and where they are, but they've been wanting and waiting to meet you officially."

"Are all of them healed? How? Healing them all would have taken longer," Oriyah asked.

"Imajin and some of the other scientists developed a solution that could be mixed with water. It worked the exact same way as the healing pool on your ship. After you drink the solution, you fall asleep and wake up the same person…just different," Aiyanna replied. "It's hard to explain."

The others chuckled as Ying added, "Yeah, we've been there."

"We have scientists now?" Elizabeth blurted.

"Yes, Imajin pushed us to use our newfound being to study physics, biology, engineering, chemistry, and mathematics. Among many other things," Prisha replied. "And now we have expanded our knowledge and are exploring ideas."

Oriyah smiled and added, "Speaking of my light, where is she?"

"Inside the training room," Aiyanna replied.

"What? How long has she been in there?" Oriyah asked.

"Ever since you sent the women you rescued from Boko Haram," Aiyanna replied.

"That long!" Oriyah exclaimed with concern. While walking briskly toward the training room, she added, "We've been gone for weeks! She can't stay in there that long. She could lose all concept of time!"

When she tried to get inside the training room, Ulloa said, "I'm sorry, but you can't go in there."

A slightly irritated Oriyah said, "And why not?"

"Because she doesn't want to be disturbed. She's made a training itinerary, and at this point it is very intense physically and mentally. If she stops now, it would all have been for nothing. This is her own choice," Ulloa replied.

"Ulloa, you know what could happen if she's in there too long!" Oriyah responded.

"Yes, I know, but she has a very good hold on things. She is in complete control." Ulloa added, "You would be impressed. Just give her time."

"Time? Give her time, while time for her moves erratically inside the simulator? For me… steady," Oriyah said with a bit of sadness. After a few groans and a long sigh, she eventually accepted the moment. "Well, she did wait a couple hundred years for me."

Ulloa added, "Exactly…Go, do what you have to do. Imajin's not going anywhere at the moment."

A frustrated Oriyah sighed. "I guess I have no choice. Since you won't let me in."

"And for that, I'm sorry," Ulloa replied.

"It's okay. I understand what she's doing," Oriyah responded. "I guess we can go ahead and make a surprise appearance at their little peace summit."

"I'm going to stay here and help out," Natalie responded.

"Oh really?" Oriyah replied.

"You're not going to meet any of the women before you leave?" Prisha replied.

"Not at the moment. We don't have much time before the summit starts," Oriyah replied.

Ying excitedly added, "Just tell them to tune in and watch us live."

"Well, before you go, we have collected some information," Prisha replied.

"Information on what?" Oriyah asked.

"Us…women," Aiyanna replied.

"And what information did you find?" Amoura asked, intrigued.

"For one thing, we found extensive knowledge of ancient women all over the world, but mainly deep beneath the ocean. It seems our history was deliberately erased and hidden from us. So we may not know our ancestor," Prisha replied.

Aiyanna interrupted: "But all that can wait! The real kicker is we took blood from everyone here before and after healing, and we found our DNA had…changed."

"It changed!" Katya exclaimed.

"Yes, it seems someone or something altered our DNA maybe thousands if not millions of years ago," Prisha replied.

Aiyanna joined in: "It's why we need them to procreate, and it's also the reason we menstruate. It's our bodies trying to correct themselves."

"And soon after the healing session, we all have started to develop abilities," Prisha added.

"Abilities like what?" Elizabeth asked.

"It varies from woman to woman, but all the children have been flourishing, with astonishing abilities, and we believe it's their youth. After Imajin and Ulloa gave us the knowledge of what we are to the universe and the celestial mother, the children, including my daughter, took to the notion like a moth to the flame," Prisha replied.

Aiyanna then added, "It seems they are who they were meant to be, and seeing that, the older women accepted the truth. God, for lack of a better word, is feminine energy. The devil is masculine. We create and they destroy." She then paused for a brief moment as the others waited for her to finish and said, "I feel so stupid. How could I actually believe I was created by a man? A man who condemns you to hell if you question him. A man who wants us to be submissive."

"Yeah, that should've been an eye-opener for all of us," Lucia replied.

"And it actually felt wrong to do so. Like, we knew we would go to hell if we didn't submit to him," Aiyanna added.

"And when you really think about it, all the movies, books, TV shows, and history have made women out to be nothing more than emotional, unstable, bitter people, and we started to believe it about one another. We cosign the male who rants about the female without thinking about what she has been through."

"And most of them have experienced the physical and mental anguish that we have," Prisha added. "Life is female."

"Well, I'm happy you finally understand," said Oriyah. "What are you going to do with that knowledge?"

"Whatever I want," Aiyanna confidently replied.

"As you should," Oriyah added.

Aiyanna then asked with slight concern, "But the real question is…what are you going to do at the summit?"

"I'm going to try a bit of diplomacy. If I don't compromise, the women of this world will suffer more than they do now, and I will not add to their pain," Oriyah replied.

"Soooo, we're just going there to talk?" Katya asked. "It won't work. They only pretend to listen."

"Well, I think it's a good idea," Natalie added. "We have laws. Without them we are no better than the animals."

Amoura replied, "That's like building a dam and disturbing the natural flow. Trying to control the natural flow of life creates chaos. Those laws you speak of favor ideas of men."

"Name one rule or law that favors men," Natalie said.

"The question is, why are their laws written specifically for women?" Farrah quipped.

They all momentarily stood in silence, waiting on Natalie's reply to a very confusing question.

"That I do not know," Natalie replied.

"I think you do, but you're not ready to admit it," Lucia replied. "But enough debate. Can we get going now before we miss the summit? I'd hate to squander this opportunity to put a little fear in the hearts of men."

"Fēmálè!" Ying said loudly.

They all paused and stared at her, wondering what was going on in her mind.

"Um, are you okay?" Farrah asked.

Ying laughed. "Yeah, I just love the way it sounds. It's like a battle cry."

They all looked at one another and smiled. Seconds later, the women started chanting, "Fēmálè! Fēmálè! Fēmálè!"

It was the beginning of a change that was so desperately needed, and it was a pleasure to almost all of them to bring about that change.

CHAPTER 18
DIPLOMACY

"Impulse control"

As things started to kick off at the UN conference building located in New York City, leaders from every country, along with a few witnesses in attendance, came together to discuss the issues, such as economic and financial woes, plaguing their countries.

The mediator from the neutral country of Switzerland started by saying, "This is an unprecedented time in our history. Never have so many countries come together to find a solution to the problems that plague our lives. Now, let's get started."

The discussion was long and tedious, with no apparent conclusion. Each country pointed fingers at the others, and no side was willing to take accountability. There always was a false sense of justifiable righteousness for a country's actions, even if they were genocidal or political. Millions across the world were tuned to listen and watch as their countries' representatives argued back and forth like bickering children.

A couple of hours into the internationally tele-vised event, as the so-called peace summit came to an end with no apparent solution to any prob-lem, a female protestor stood up and shouted, "So no talk about the mistreatment of women around the world? Even though sex trafficking, domestic abuse, and child marriage are at an all-time high? Or the fact that the word woman is considered offensive?" She then added, "I guess that's not a problem to you."

"We don't have the time. There are more im-portant matters to attend to," an American repre-sentative, a trans woman named Rachel, replied.

"It might not matter to you. But it matters to us. We have become mere afterthoughts or spoils of war. We are either raped and enslaved or raped and murdered. We are tired of it!" She exclaimed. "Have all the wars you want. You can all kill one another for all I care, but leave women out of it. Just leave us alone."

"Security, remove her from the room, please," the mediator said.

"Remove me for speaking the truth?!" she re-plied as more than a few security guards surrounded her while aggressively attempting to remove her from the area.

Without warning, a portal opened behind the mediator as he stood near the podium. The audience members gasped in shock as they watched beings emerge covered from the neck down in silver and specks of gold. The nanite-infused bodysuits seemingly vibrated as they flickered in the sun peering through the window, while their hooded capes, white with gold trim, reflected the sunlight, creating a visible aura of energy around the group of women, and as the portal closed behind them, the kaleidoscope of colors slowly dissipated. The bright sun retreated behind the clouds as if their presence were its sole reason for departing, just so the rays could shine through at that very moment.

However, the attendees were momentarily caught in the marvel of glorious importance, each of them linking the miraculous event to religious providence—that is, up until the figures' faces were revealed to be those of a pack of females whose mere presence was a projection of a strong will and a whole bunch of power that made the testicles of every man in the room retreat into his stomach. It was a fear that caused every man's ego to react without learning or understanding.

Before asking a question, the guards drew their firearms and aimed them directly at the women.

"Freeze—don't move!" they shouted while aggressively approaching them.

"Hands on your heads, and get down on your knees!" the guards yelled.

"We come in peace," Oriyah stated as they continued to yell over her.

Noticing they didn't care whether or not she was peaceful, Oriyah slowly raised her hands, seemingly complying with their demands. Then she suddenly snapped her fingers, an act that sent a shock wave throughout the entire room, before tossing a spherical object into the air that attached itself to the ceiling. It drew every weapon to it like a magnet, disarming the trigger-happy males and at the same time inciting panic in the room.

"React first, ask questions later. The male ego in a nutshell," Ying whispered over the communicator as they listened and watched the panicked faces of men and women alike. Oriyah could have treated them as they had treated her. But diplomacy demanded patience, so impulse was unwarranted. She approached the podium and attempted to calm the crowd by shushing it like a frustrated teacher in a class of unruly children.

"My name," she yelled over their panicky cries to focus their attention before returning to her normal tone, "is Oriyah. I am the daughter of Mayri, daughter of Asherah, one of the first females to inhabit this planet. I understand this is all quite shocking, but we're not here to harm anyone or cause any trouble."

"Yet," Ying jokingly whispered over the radio as they stood side by side behind their leader.

"We just want to talk. So please just hear me out," Oriyah continued.

"They're not going to listen. They're probably thinking of ways to kill you," Katya added to the whispers over their communicators.

Seconds later, a bullet from a guard who still had a weapon struck her chest before the gun flew from his hand, joining the others now attached to the spherical object in the air.

She peeled the flattened bullet from her chest completely unfazed and tossed it back at the guard. A complete feeling of inadequacy fell over the man who had pulled the trigger.

Oriyah shook her head with more frustration before taking a deep breath, calming the anger inside, and saying calmly, "Your society tells women what they can and cannot do or be, while almost every culture tells them they're not good enough. I'm here to tell them they can do whatever they want and they are good enough. I'm here to give them a safe space to live and thrive, free from patriarchal rule and ideals."

"What do you mean?" the lady who was being removed from the room asked.

"This world is not set up for females to live. It's set up for them to just survive. So we have procured some land for women only. A place where we're free to live. Everything that is provided for you will be by you. No resources are needed from any country. Currency or money is not needed for anything. We will teach you who and what you are! If any woman wants to come, you are more than welcome. We will come get you if necessary," Oriyah answered.

"What about husbands, fathers, brothers, and—?" she asked before she was cut off midsentence by a very stern answer.

"Not allowed, nor will they ever be. This is a male-free zone. A no-man's-land plain and simple," Oriyah said, with an intense stare that meant every word.

"Why not?" an Afghani representative asked.

"Our choice," she replied. "That's all that matters."

"Do you hate men?" the US president asked.

"Hate? No, I just know what you are, even if you don't," she replied.

"Well, despite what you may feel about us, you can't just come here and set up shop. We have laws and procedures here. A little thing called checks and balances," he replied sarcastically as some of the audience members agreed, forgetting for the moment that a snap of her fingers could probably kill them. Ego, getting the best of man once again.

"And sharing resources is something we do on this planet," another man added.

A slightly irritated Oriyah replied, "We are going to help the planet, and in return that helps all of us."

"How!?" a Chinese rep boldly asked.

"Our scientists have already developed a way to thoroughly clean the oceans. But we need you all to stop dumping your trash and toxic barrels so we can reverse the damage done," she answered.

"That doesn't sound like much," China's representative replied.

"We're open to sharing technology that can tap into your world energy grid. Wireless energy for everyone and medical cures for whatever ails you," she added.

"What are you all wearing? What about that portal-like thing you all came from?" he replied.

"Nanite-infused biosuits. Also for females only!" she exclaimed. "I will not give you the knowledge to create a portal. Giving you the means to travel anywhere in the world instantly would not be good for the planet."

"Why should women be the only ones with that power?!" North Korea's president joined in.

"Because it's been proven that males with power yearn for more power," she sternly replied.

"What about trans women?" blurted a woman in the audience whose friend, standing beside her, was a trans woman in full agreement with her question, as was the American trans rep.

"What about them?" Elizabeth interrupted while standing behind Oriyah.

"Are they invited?" Oriyah replied.

"Why would they be? They're men!" Elizabeth said with confidence.

"I'm both, I'm better, I'm beyond," the woman's trans friend replied.

"If that is what you believe, then that is your right. But that doesn't mean I have to!" Elizabeth replied with a look in her eye that would send shivers down your spine.

"That's a conversation for another time," Iran's representative added before directing his question to Oriyah: "Is that all you want?"

"Release all female political prisoners, stop forcing women into prostitution, and stop the sex trade, or I will do it myself. If any woman wants to leave her current location, she shall not be harmed," Oriyah quickly replied, seemingly done with the whole charade.

Iran's rep chuckled and said, "None of our women will join you or your little cult of whatever you are!"

India's representative shouted, "This is our world. You can't just come here and tell us what to do."

"I don't think you understand how things work here," the Russian president added with a smug look upon his face as the others chucked and mumbled in agreement. Even in the face of a power greater than their own, pride and ego could not be suppressed. It was the nature of the male when looking at a woman.

Oriyah looked around the room, and with a smug smile of her own, she added, "Listen. I told you my mother and her mother are from your world. However, I am not! I come from a world where females from all over the universe and several dimensions reside, living peacefully. Yes, we have our individual squabbles, but nobody dies. Nobody is bought and sold, like the strong women standing behind me, for pleasure to any sadist, rapist, or pedophile. Nobody is set on fire, stoned, or murdered for learning. No woman worries about beauty standards or the validation of males, and little girls aren't forced to marry adult men. The fact that you're trying to legalize relations with children and make little girl robots for sexual pleasure tells me all I need to know about the direction of your world. So let's get something very clear."

She said, emotionless, "To me, you're a pathetic bunch of beings not worth the lives you're living. An invasive species that disrupts natural flow. Agents of chaos, a destructive deviant that needs to end for the universe to thrive. I care nothing about you, but I will never harm a female, and a lot of the women here have an almost unwavering need for the likes of you in their lives, and you've convinced them that intimately loving another woman is a sin." She chuckled condescendingly and added, "Your religions are funny. I get a good laugh out of them—well, most of them. Good job, by the way. You purposely made women submissive servants in every way, and they choose not to see it, but…that is their choice. Ours is for the women who want true freedom." She ended her rant with the words "No more."

Seconds later, a few of the nations knew exactly what those words meant. Because it was the phrase found in a few locations where men had been left mangled and defiled.

"You!!!" an Afghani representative shouted. "My brother was among those men you murdered!"

"By definition, murder is one human killing another," Farrah blurted, "and you're a demon."

"I am a man, God's son," he passionately replied.

"Yes, you are…your God is the devil. So that means you're a demon," Farrah confidently replied with a deathly stare.

The man grew more livid by the second. Not only because of his slain brother but also because this woman was speaking in a tone of no respect and disrespecting his entire culture. Before long his pride got the best of him. He then said in a demeaning tone, "And you are nothing. You were made for me by me. It was our rib that gave you life."

Immediately after that statement, in full view of the world watching, she dashed toward him, and with a powerful blow, she struck him in the side, then said, "Now that rib is broken." The room instantly erupted in panic. As she went back to join her sisters, she glanced at Oriyah and mouthed the word "Sorry," knowing this was supposed to be a diplomatic approach.

Oriyah shook her head and raised her hand, and the crowd went silent because everyone knew a snap of the fingers could be on the way. She said, "No trespassing, no flyovers, no satellites or drones near our lands. We will not trade or share technology or agriculture. We are our own, on our own. No men, no exceptions."

"And you're seriously going to exclude trans women?" the trans rep yelled.

Elizabeth groaned loudly and said, "You don't give up, do you!"

A female UK representative added, "Look, there's a whole community of people who feel the way she does. I think it would be progressive and diplomatic to allow them to at least be able to visit. Here trans women are women."

"So you agree with him?" Oriyah asked.

"I'm not a him; I'm a she," the trans woman shouted angrily before the UK rep had a chance to answer.

Elizabeth laughed and said, "We've been reduced to a feeling."

"What did you say?" The trans woman replied with a demanding tone of voice.

Each of them was slightly shocked at the rep's tone, and all of them looked at Elizabeth, waiting for her response. She glared at the protestor and said, "A man who feels like a woman." She chuckled and added, "The ignorance of thinking being a woman is a feeling is very…manlike."

"I'm a woman!" the trans woman shouted.

"No the heck you're not!" Elizabeth added. "You're an imitation, a knockoff, far from the real thing. You think putting on a dress and some makeup and twirling around like an idiot while flipping your hair around makes you a woman!? You're a cross-dresser. Plain and simple."

"Damn, that was cold," Ying said out loud, forgetting to whisper, making the trans woman angrier than before. The male ego. It never falters. No matter what you identify as.

"Bitch, you're nothing compared to me. I'm better than you at being you. You're just another TERF!" the trans woman replied.

"Well, since I'm a TERF, currently on your turf, I have a question for you," Elizabeth added.

In the blink of an eye, her hand was around the trans woman's throat as the trans woman frantically grabbed at her hand, trying to pry it from her throat, before realizing the obvious difference in strength.

Without notice, the nanites sliced perfectly around her neck, releasing an arterial spray of blood on everyone nearby.

While watching the life drain from the trans woman's eyes, Elizabeth said, "What do you feel now?" as she began to pull off the trans woman's head with the spinal cord still attached.

The crowd gasped in horror, as some were covered in blood. Others were vomiting from the sheer stomach-churning mess in front of them. While glaring at the UK rep, Elizabeth tossed the severed head toward her feet and said, "That's for you since you want to sympathize with them while they erase us."

The panic in the room became uncontrollable as Oriyah mumbled to herself, "I guess diplomacy is done," forgetting for the moment that her sisters could hear her.

"Finally," Ying reacted excitedly as she readied her weapons.

"No!" Oriyah shouted as a portal opened near them. "Let's go."

Just as she said that, the doors exploded, breached by soldiers ready to do their duty. The headless body on the floor and the broken ribs of an important man were more than enough of a reason for them to take up arms, an action that was pretty much inevitable.

The soldiers started immediately firing, striking the individual energy force fields created by the women's wrist gauntlets.

"Can we kill them now!?!" Lucia exclaimed as the bullets struck their shields.

"Yeah, this is a good moment to showcase our strength," Farrah added.

"You just ripped off a representative's head. I think they know," Oriyah replied. "Let's go!" she added as they moved backward one by one through the portal.

CHAPTER 19
WAR

"Sometimes it's good for something"

B ack on the ship, headed toward home base, there was an awkward silence in the room. Nobody said a word as Oriyah stood silently with a fixed gaze upon both Farrah and Elizabeth, like a disappointed parent getting ready to scold a child for something she wanted to or would've done herself.

After a long uncomfortable moment of silence and a scathing stare, Farrah said, "Sorry, but he was rude. At least I didn't make a mess, unlike some people," referring to Elizabeth.

They all started snickering as Oriyah still stood there without an ounce of emotion on her face. She then added, "Well, what's your excuse?"

Like a child contemplating what lie to tell, she replied, "He…Ummmm…had a gun. Yeah! He had a gun. I thought he was going to try and shoot you like the other guy. I was protecting my sister, my mentor, my friend."

Everyone except Oriyah the parent burst into laughter.

"She's right! I saw it too. He had a gun," Ying jokingly replied.

Oriyah shook her head, trying to contain her own laughter. "I don't know what to say," she added.

"Aww, I know you wanted to do it yourself," Katya teased.

Her comment was met with a grin and a wink signifying she had thought about doing it herself.

"This was supposed to be a diplomatic effort," she added.

"Diplomacy to men is other people doing what they say, and I'm not doing that anymore," Katya replied.

Lucia suddenly joined in, "We tried to tell you that they wouldn't listen. We've lived here all our lives. We know how they are."

"I understand that, but now it will be an all-out war, and other women will pay the price," Oriyah replied.

"War is inevitable if there is to be change on a massive scale," Katya added. "We've been talking for years. Words don't work here. Actions are the only thing they hear."

"Other women will see man's true nature. Then they will realize that their religions are a lie. We are not property or servants. We are not bitches and hoes. We don't need their validation, and we don't need them," Farrah added.

"Whoop, whoop!" Ying shouted in agreement with her statement. "I believe a lot more than you think will join us, and our little piece of home will become a metropolis for women only."

"What a beautiful thought," Lucia replied. "It's poetic, really."

"What is?" Ying asked.

"Men created the circumstances for their own demise," she replied.

Oriyah looked into the eyes of her companions and saw the passion that screamed change, as if a locomotive with no brakes pulling the weight of years of abuse and violence was now an unstoppable force of irony that would be man's eventual downfall.

"They should all be dead. Or at least 95 to 99 percent," Katya added.

"Or 99.9999," Farrah replied, as the others joined in repeating ".999999999999."

They started laughing joyfully like literal sisters who had shared the same womb. Maternal twins with solidified bonds that couldn't be broken.

"FĒMÁLÈ!" Oriyah responded before they all simultaneously shouted the word together.

They were riled up and ready for what was to come. Man had been winning the battle for millennia, but the war was yet to come. A few women evolving their devolving had started to tip the balance of male kind's unbalance. If every woman could make that change, what would the possibilities be? But the true question was, would the rest of the women on Earth make that change, or was the grip of man's hold on their minds and spirits too strong to pry open?

A few seconds later, their cheers were interrupted by damning alerts coming from home base.

"Ulloa, what's going on?!?" Oriyah exclaimed with concern.

"Home base is currently under attack," she responded.

"What?! How is that? We have a twenty-mile security perimeter around the entire base?!?" Oriyah exclaimed.

"Imajin…somehow she locked me out of my own system. So as not to disturb you while you were at the summit," Ulloa responded.

"How is that even possible?" Oriyah asked.

"I don't know," Ulloa replied. "But she and a few others are dealing with problems as we speak."

"Where are they now?" Oriyah asked.

Moments later the ship projected a holographic visual of Imajin and the other women in the midst of combat, right where the snowy tundra met the jungle like oasis they called home. It was a battle of man-made machines versus women in biosuits. A battle the machines being operated by men were losing terribly.

Caught in amazement, they watched as a small but sizable force of tanks, Apache helicopters, and unmanned remote-controlled drones rained down a barrage of bullets and Hellfire missiles on the group of women.

However, the most shocking part, at least to Oriyah, was Imajin's mental intensity and phys-ical prowess. She used her biosuit as a literal extension of herself, constructing weapons with ease simultaneously as she moved with a speed so fast the live feed could barely keep up. She trampled snow Humvees equipped with fifty-caliber machine guns like they were a child's playthings. Armored explosive-round-carrying tanks telekinetically imploded as the sounds of muffled bloodcurdling screams from crushed men resonated from within. She launched beams of light from her hands that sliced through the clouds and fighter jets alike.

Oriyah gushed at the abilities and tenacity of a female who had once thought her strength was nonexistent. A female who had believed her only worth was what others had forced her to believe.

Free from the chaos that had plagued her past, she was able to break through the shell of self-doubt, an act that released the potential of a daughter of the celestial mother. As the celestial mother's child, she should have been familiar with the word limitless.

Meanwhile, caught in the symphony of beautiful destruction, none of them knew the ship had landed on the roof of one of the four buildings at their home base until they heard the explosions and rapid gunfire, which made them realize they could now see the battle with their own eyes.

They rushed outside and saw helicopters and UAVs alike knocked from the sky by an array of energy projectiles from wrist gauntlets. With a clear view of the battlefield, they watched intently as their sisters dismembered a squadron of infantrymen while others sought out snipers on the hillside dressed in all white, blending in with the snowy tundra. They fought and moved like a team in perfect sync, positively feeding off one another.

The winners of the unexpected scuffle were obvious. It must've become obvious to the soldiers as well, because some of them threw down their weapons and ran for the hills.

Maybe it was the sizzling flesh from the men caught in downed aircraft or the broken and separated body parts that riddled the battlefield, or it could possibly have been the blood-covered snow with scattered entrails that painted a horrible picture of the conclusion of the day's events.

Truth was, not one man on the planet saw it coming: women making men feel completely powerless while standing together strong, with an unmatched intelligence and unwavering ferocity that men could never comprehend. Either way, the soldiers were in full retreat, with their tails tucked between their legs like scared puppies.

After all was done, Imajin and her fighters themselves withdrew from the battlefield and re-grouped within the force field that protected their home.

Anxious to get a close-up of her new being, Oriyah walked off the edge of the roof and did not fall.

"I knew you could fly," Ying said excitedly.

She smiled and said "Of course I can—it's just more fun to run" as she flew toward Imajin.

After reaching their location, she saw Imajin covered in blood and soot from the flames. She looked into her eyes as her body started to glow and emit a source of heat comparable to the flames itself. The debris covering her body vanished into nothing, leaving her biosuit as pristine as the day she put it on.

In complete amazement, Oriyah asked, "What happened to you?"

"You," Imajin replied with a smile before run-ning to leap into her arms. She kissed her gently on lips and added, "And I shared you with them."

"I don't understand," Oriyah replied.

Still in her arms, Imajin said, "You remember when you let me see into your mind back home?"

"Yes," Oriyah replied.

"You also remember I told you it was something I didn't fully understand, right?" Imajin added.

"Ummmm…yes," Oriyah repeated.

"Apparently, when I did that, some of you poured into me. Your past, your knowledge and skill. All of it!" Imajin explained. "That's why I locked myself away. I needed to figure it out. It was a painful mental and physical process, but I overcame it. I learned the core of a female is compassion, but compassion is only the trunk of the tree. The branches are her intellect, the stems are her ferocity, and the leaves are her story, and they bloom in the light and night alike. She is the tree of life."

Unexpectedly, a portal opened behind them as some of the other sisters rushed through, shoving a bound Natalie before them.

"It was her! She gave them our location," Amoura yelled. Commotion immediately broke out in shock and disapproval.

"What? Why?!" Oriyah exclaimed.

After a brief pause, Natalie said passionately, "I love my father, my grandfather, and my brothers. I will not stand by and watch you murder them." She then continued, "I understand you all have been through hell, but this is not the way. We need men, and they need us." To the other women, she said, "They're basically aliens telling us our history is false. Don't let an alien tell you what it means to be human."

Her words fell on deaf ears—these women were sisters, and they would not be held down by mankind anymore. They would not be swayed.

"In the words of Assata Shakur, 'Nobody in the word, nobody in history, has ever got their freedom by appealing to the moral sense of the people who were oppressing them,'" Amoura angrily replied as her biosuit constructed a long axe fit for beheading. "You betrayed us."

"No!" Oriyah shouted. "We don't do that to one of our own. Untie her, free her from any technology she received from us, and send her home."

"Wait, really? That's it?!?" Natalie asked, as if she were skeptical or maybe a little shocked.

Without warning a barrage of explosions went off in rapid succession. A different kind of weaponry, something other than primitive man-made machinery, was impacting the force field. The strike was enough to create a small hole big enough for a platoon to fit through before closing on its own, repairing the damage.

Suddenly a ship using a tactic they'd used themselves appeared out of thin air. It slowly descended from the sky before a beam of light struck the ground and a few dozen creatures who were not human males materialized.

Large, vicious-looking reptile like creatures who bore an array of gadgetry, along with disgusting blood-and-dirt-ridden razor-sharp claws and fangs, glared at them with malicious intent. Their black eyes showed no fear, just a want for fresh meat. The kind that wiggles when you eat it.

It seemed their actions had forced what had been hiding in the dark to reveal itself to the light. A woman in control of her own was something male kind of all origins secretly feared, and that fear had been noticed.

"Finally a challenge," Oriyah responded as she began her stride toward the action. "Let's get to work."

"Wait!" Imajin shouted.

"What's wrong?" Oriyah replied while rushing to her side.

"Something feels different," she said. "Something strong is coming."

"What's that in the distance behind the ship?" Katya asked. "It's like a massive snowstorm coming this way."

"That's random," Ying replied.

Suddenly, Ulloa joined in: "I don't think it's random at all. I'm reading approximately eight heat signatures within the storm."

"Who could that be?" said Oriyah.

Whoever or whatever it may have been was enough to catch the attention of every one of the creatures currently preparing to attack. Without hesitation they ran toward the storm as the ship launched a bombardment of energy projectiles into the center of the storm. Within seconds the storm engulfed the ship and creatures alike.

Moments later, a bright light went off from inside the storm. Suddenly the ship imploded and disintegrated into nothing. Following that, pain-filled shrieking reverberated loudly from inside the wind and snow. Before long it was raining mangled bodies and body parts that struck the sides of the force field, leaving trails of black blood as they slowly slid down toward the ground.

Shortly afterward, the shrieking stopped. The only thing to be heard was the wind and snow as it continued to move toward their location. When the storm reached the outer perimeter, it stopped and dissipated. Exactly eight people dressed in rags like common hobos, with sunglasses and ski masks, stood motionless for a brief moment while looking their way.

A few seconds later, one of them placed a hand upon the force field, which created a hole big enough for the eight of them to fit though. This action caused a few of the sisters to ready their weapons, but even then the people continued to approach.

Now they were no more than a few feet away. It seemed they were all staring at Oriyah. Then only one of them suddenly said, "Mayri, is that you?"

"No," Oriyah replied, "Mayri is my mother's name."

"You look exactly like her," one of them replied.

Following that, all of them took off their sunglasses and masks, revealing themselves to be women also.

Afterward they all said their names, which were Yemaya, Guadalupe, Eve, Durga, Amaterasu, Guanyin, Sedna, and Lilith.

Heaven being a community of different cultures and races, each of the women listening knew these names oh so well—some from myth and legend, others from folklore and religion.

"Her sisters," Oriyah replied, shocked. "How can this be? She thinks you're dead!"

"We're not, but it's been a very hard millennium," Eve joked, with sadness in her eyes held at bay by willpower alone.

"Where is she?" Durga asked.

"On another planet far from here. I can take you if you'd like. It would brighten her life to see you again," Oriyah replied.

"We would love that!" Lilith exclaimed joyfully.

A split second later, Imajin dropped to her knees in apparent pain. Oriyah rushed to her side and said with concern, "What's wrong?!?"

After a brief pause in the midst of trying to catch her breath, she shakenly replied, "Something strong is coming. Something bad!"

Almost immediately after that statement, unexpectedly the ground started to violently shake and rumble like an earthquake. The once clear blue sky turned red like the clouds themselves were bleeding. Previously undisturbed snow melted rapidly as volcanic fissures rose from the ground, spewing magma and sulfur in every direction. Dozens of lightning strikes struck the ground within seconds as deafening thunder rattled the stone mountains in the distance. The air itself turned stale while the very frequency of the world itself shifted, altering the flow of the planet.

Suddenly the ground started giving way. Dirt and rock sank into a hole with seemingly no bottom.

Afterward, a monstrous hand with long black fingernails reached out and clawed at the ground above. Then a loud roar, followed by a wall of fire, exploded from the dark pit, and a loud demonic voice called out, "Daughters of the first. I've been looking for you."

The fires slowly receded, revealing a nightmarish demonic entity. A being so terrifying that if you dreamed about it, you'd never sleep again. As if its intimidating aura and long horns weren't enough, its upper body also looked as though it had been skinned and burned.

Its teeth were as black as obsidian, while its blood red eyes held pitch-black pupils as dark as the void in between the stars. Large bat-like wings with barbs along the shoulders and a snake for a tail gave the horrifying demon a more visually frightening demeanor.

CHAPTER 20
REVELATION—I.E., JUDGMENT DAY

"Daughter of Mayri Magdalene"

"He's come back again," Eve responded as the demon stood motionless while staring at them with a distasteful grin upon its face and sadism in its posture.

"And who is he?" Oriyah asked while glaring into the eyes of the monstrous creature.

"The one who took Mayri from us," Durga replied as they readied their weapons.

"We vanquished him five times, and he just keeps coming back," Guanyin angrily added.

"He's relentless, and the more they praise him, the stronger he becomes. The last time we barely survived," Amaterasu joined in.

"We can take him again!" Yemaya and Guadalupe said in unison.

The sisters were visibly shaken by his sudden appearance. Hidden fear and a dose of doubt consumed their minds as their hearts beat ten times faster than usual. They seemed discouraged by the task ahead, but their instincts prepared them for battle. It was clear this was a fight they did not want, but it was indeed the fight in front of them.

Suddenly, the demon took off into the air at blinding speed before abruptly stopping and hovering in place. He stretched out his arms and legs as if he were just waking up from a good nap. He then returned his menacing gaze back upon the sisters while flicking his snakelike tongue in and out.

All of a sudden, his huge wings wrapped around his body like those of a sleeping bat. For a few seconds, everything went completely quiet.

In anticipation Sedna said, "What is he doing?"

Without warning, his wings burst open with a force so great it created a tremendous shock wave that rippled across the valley floor, temporarily disabling the force field.

Imajin looked at the faces of her sisters and saw a fear so deeply embedded into their psyches it momentarily severed their instincts. Now they stood frozen in panic and afraid to act. However, with Oriyah it was the complete opposite. She had a look on her face like she was trying to hold back a joyful smile, which would have been a clear sign of her excitement for this moment.

At the same time, she felt pent-up anger for a man she wanted to punish, but that man was no more. Vengeance could not be had in a world where he did not exist, a world where his existence and martyrdom permeated an entire planet, and that truth was an annoyance to the very core of her rage, a rage that tempted her to go against everything she believed. The human woman and the human male…for a moment, her intention was to kill them all. However, now her intentions were pure, and the source of her anger had physical form.

With a curious stare and punitive intent, Oriyah peered at the demon as he continued hovering in the air. She slowly took off her wrist gauntlet and hooded cloak before handing them over to Imajin and saying, "Whatever happens, do not interfere."

"What? No! You can't fight him alone!!!" Guanyin exclaimed.

"He is too powerful!" Durga added with surety.

Without uttering a single word, Oriyah slowly ascended into the sky toward the demon.

"I can't lie. This is a fight I'm anxious to see," Ying added as the others agreed.

Mayri's sisters looked at her with disappointed scowls on their faces.

"I'm sorry, but you have to see the things she can do," Ying respectfully responded.

"We can't let her fight him alone," Lilith insisted.

"We would get in the way," Imajin interrupted. She then explained, "nearly two thousand years she's been training to be her mother. Then on the day of her birth and the end of her training, she learns of her mother's hidden pain and finds out that pain is connected to her dreams, and it's all connected to him. She needs this before she moves on. If we helped, she'd only end up killing one of us by mistake."

She then took a moment to reflect on the sheer intensity of Oriyah's energy, and with a smirk she added, "Plus, it's fun for her."

Meanwhile, Oriyah and the demonic entity were face to face merely a few meters away from each other. The massive energy of two opposing forces felt destructive. However, only one was destructive by nature. The other was on the path of destruction.

She examined his form, curious about the creature, before returning her gaze back upon his blood red eyes and black, hole-like pupils.

With the same distasteful grin and sadistic eyes, he said to her in a long, deep demonic tone, "Are you familiar to me, woman?"

With an ominous tone and threatening manner, she replied while inching her way toward him, "Well, that depends. What's your name?"

"We've had many names. We've lived many lives," the demon answered as his snake tail moved hypnotically above his head.

"I'm only interested in one," she replied.

"Ra!" he said before unexpectedly striking her across the face in an attack that had so much force it sent her flying backward toward the ground. The impact itself produced a crater a couple of meters wide and a few feet deep.

"Ganesh!" he shouted while descending on top of her with his hooves first, stomping down on her chest with a blow greater than the previous.

"Zeus!" he added as he returned to the sky.

He chuckled lightly, pleased with his work, as he hovered in place, waiting for her to emerge. He then continued, "Mephistopheles, Lucifer, Vish-nu, Anubis, Yah, Weh…Yahweh."

Oriyah slowly ascended from the center of the crater while dusting the debris from her shoulders, apparently unfazed by his sneak attack.

"Impressive," he responded as she rejoined him in the sky.

After a brief pause of deep thought, the demon said, "We've lived for thousands of years among humanity, reaping the benefits of a physical form, and only once have we come close to perishing." He then added, as his snakelike tongue licked his lips, "We know who you are," as if the thought of his actions brought back arousing memories.

"What is your name?" Oriyah replied nonchalantly, disregarding his attempt to entice her to react.

Ignoring her question, he continued, "Being healed in that cave gave me the capabilities I now enjoy. The capability to move throughout the cosmos wherever life is present and become a god in the eyes of the impressionable. Their prayers and praise are my nourishment."

"What is your name?" she repeated.

The demon of many names chuckled and descended to the ground. He then said, "Abaddon, Set, Hades, Sango, Muhammad, Buddha." It was clear he knew the name she sought, but withholding that one name was the power of control, an aphrodisiac for the ego.

Boom! A loud, thunderous noise resonated throughout the area. It was the result of a strike to the gut of the demon, buckling his goat like legs before a powerful uppercut sent him flying into the air.

Oriyah was looking to the sky with her hands clasped behind her back. She emanated a vibe that presented strength and will while being devoid of fear and doubt. She waited patiently for the monster to return.

Suddenly a loud roar from the livid demon, followed by a dark gathering of energy, came from behind the clouds. Seconds later, a long streak of black light rushed toward her, and the fight officially began.

They moved with the speed of a single blink, while each blow sounded like bombs exploding one by one, but the movements of Oriyah were neither offensive or defensive. Was she testing the limit of his power, frozen from fear, or was she still waiting for a specific name?

However, the demonic creature was indeed relentless, going all in on a destructive attack. Using all abilities he possessed, like the monster he was, he ferociously pummeled her without end while growling and foaming at the mouth like a rabid dog. His wings lacerated her flesh, cutting through her biosuit, while his fist collided with her face and head. At the same time, his snake tail struck her body repeatedly, injecting venom into her blood.

A couple of minutes later, in the midst of a horrific beating, Oriyah said emotionlessly to the demon, "What is your name?"

He roared loudly in complete rage, loathing the sheer nerve of this being who was seemingly unmoved by her own injuries and even more unmoved by the power he possessed.

"Anu, Shamash, Horus!" he shouted angrily before striking her again violently, knocking her to the ground.

Immediately afterward, the demon of many names conjured some dark energy and made a lightning bolt that screamed with the souls of the damned. He then added "My reign, my likeness, is everywhere" and threw it at her with such force that it scorched the air as it moved. After it made contact with her chest, a huge explosion of petrified souls that spread like black smoke shook the entire continent.

The demon laughed joyfully, pleased with the chaos he'd created. Meanwhile, Oriyah's companions were very worried and tempted to enter the intense battle. The cloud of screaming souls that continued to expand while engulfing their force field, as well the earth shaking beneath their feet, was beginning to force their hand.

All of a sudden, the ground stopped moving, the black cloud stopped expanding, and everything went silent. Only the maniacal laughter of the demon of many names could be heard. That is, until the screaming souls started humming among themselves. He noticed a light within the point of impact and watched as it gradually spread and altered the very fabric of the dark cloud, making it shine brighter than the sun itself, while the trapped souls within took to the cosmos, free of their torment.

As the demon looked around in confusion, a feeling in the air made him realize Oriyah was behind him. It was an act that startled the monstrous being, something that he himself had never felt.

She had lacerations across her face and body, and he observed the blood sliding down her biosuit. Burned flesh from the lightning bolt covered her chest, and venom from snake bites leaked from their wounds. He knew she should be in pain, but neither her posture nor the look in her eyes radiated that claim.

She then said with an innocent smile, "My mother's pain," as her injuries rapidly started to heal on their own. She then added, "The trapped souls of females can be freed by other females. They're free now."

"Plenty more where those came from," He confidently replied. "They give me their souls without question."

"All those female souls," Oriyah responded while stretching as if she were getting ready for a short jog. She then stopped and said, while looking into the black pits of his eyes, "And you're still so weak. I thought you'd be a challenge, but you're too frightened of me to tell me your name."

"We're afraid of nothing," he replied as his body began to shake with anger. The gall of this woman talking down to a being who saw himself as above it all. The core of his black heart was aching to lash out.

Prior to his ego's prideful reaction, Oriyah said calmly, with a straight face, "I wonder if demonic entities like you can feel pain or the fear of not existing." She smiled and added, "Get ready. We're about to find out."

Within a split second, a barrage of various strikes in rapid succession overwhelmed the not-so-imposing figure in an attack that humiliated the image he had of himself.

His snake for a tail was torn off with her bare hands, along with a single wing, which disabled his flying capabilities. She watched and grinned as he fell from the sky like a literal bat out of hell.

Before he had a chance to rise from his downfall, she picked him up by his remaining wing and began to break bones while powerful body blows forced a flood of tar-like blood to flow profusely from the creature's mouth.

His attempt to counter was rewarded with the snapping off of both horns. In a degrading act, one was jammed into his eye, while the other was stuffed into the hole where his tail used to be. It was a humiliating tactic for the so-called alphas, learned from her human female companions.

After the horn to the hole and a quick strike to the solar plexus, which brought the demon to his knees, she ceased her violent attack and said teasingly, "Did you feel any of that? Do you feel your existence slipping away at the hands of your karma?" She knew that he knew the name she sought, but his reluctance to say it was like a piece of hair stuck in her eye. Non-life-threatening but very irritating.

Beaten and battered, with missing limbs and a tarnished ego, the demon replied with a mouth full of blood, "You don't get it, you little bitch! We are not one…"

Moments later, the sky shifted from red to a shade resembling the void of space. The air itself began to vibrate as a feeling of danger compelled even Oriyah to take a step back. The broken demon began to rise as twelve dark spheres that mirrored a miniature black hole appeared and gathered around him. His severed appendages grew back, and his gaping wounds healed as the dark spheres spread out, engulfing his body. "We are many!" the demon said as they covered him completely, leaving a black, misshapen bubble of dark energy that steadily decreased in size while increasing its density.

Immediately afterward, ill-lit, unusual bolts of lightning rapidly struck the ground as the clouds themselves were set ablaze. Multiple voices in different tones, all speaking separate languages, whispered from within the darkness of the sphere.

"We are…Legion."

Suddenly the dark ball of chaotic energy started to take form as it continued, with a multitude of voices speaking simultaneously, "In persona Christi, Yeshua. He is us; we are him; we are many."

"Finally!" Oriyah annoyingly blurted in the midst of his transformation. "You had to make it a mystery."

Like any conceited, self-centered, self-serving, narcissistic, egotistical, maniacal control freak, Legion replied in a long, guttural tone, "Ex opere operato…We are the mystery. We work in mysterious ways."

Oriyah laughed loudly, mocking the demon as all hell broke loose around her, and said, "Male kind in a nutshell. It seems all of you are delusional."

The end.
Or is it his end?
Her beginning?
To be continued…

Milton Keynes UK
Ingram Content Group UK Ltd.
UKHW021952281024
450365UK00013B/679

9 798822 948723